I0617146

Stronger than the Storm
Hurricane Helene in Western North Carolina

Edited and with an Introduction
by Shelley McKechnie

☙HAW CREEK PRESS

Asheville, North Carolina USA

2025

First Edition

Cover illustration from *Taking Flight* by Kimberly Smith.

ISBN: 979-8-9922037-0-7
Library of Congress Control Number: 2025900392

To the helpers

To the people of western North Carolina,
Together we will rebuild

To those affected by severe weather events,
past, present, and future

Stronger than the Storm: Hurricane Helene in Western North Carolina

Table of Contents

Table of Contents

Introduction

On September 26, 2024, Category 4 Hurricane Helene made landfall in Florida, then traveled hundreds of miles inland. The next morning it arrived as a tropical storm in the mountains and valleys of already rain-soaked western North Carolina. It's where I live.

It created utter devastation. It broke records here that are hard to grasp, and help put in context the work you'll see in this book:

▶ At several area weather stations, rainfall from the storm and the preceding few days exceeded 20 inches. A station in Yancey County recorded 30.78 inches of rainfall.[1] That's only 4.19 inches less than Sea-Tac Airport in Seattle WA got in *all* of 2023.[2]

▶ Rains travel down mountains to feed the creeks and rivers that flow through towns. Depending on location, flood level starts between 9.5 and 13 feet[3,4]. The Swannanoa River crested at 27.33 feet at Biltmore in Asheville[5]. Nearby, it meets the French Broad River which rose to 24.67 feet[3]. In Fletcher, The French Broad crested at 30.39[4] feet. That's roughly the height of a three-story building.

▶ Water speed turbocharged the destruction. In the Appalachian Trail town of Hot Springs, where Spring Creek meets the French Broad River, the French Broad "pulsed at 101,000 cubic feet per second — equal to the amount of water flowing over Niagara Falls in high season and ten times stronger than the Class IV rapids in the Colorado River at the Grand Canyon, considered some of the most challenging in the U.S."[6]

▶ Peak wind gusts at several weather stations topped 60mph. To get a sense of that, consider how it feels when you stick your hand out the car window while driving down the highway. Then imagine the impact at nearby Mt. Mitchell, where gusts reached 106 mph.[1]

▶ In the Southern Appalachian region, there were more than 2,000 landslides. Most were in western North Carolina.[7]

▶ Three months after the storm the death toll in North Carolina stands at 104. Forty-two of those are from here in Buncombe County.[8] It seems everyone here either knows someone who died or is within two degrees of separation.

▶ In the region's Nantahala and Pisgah National Forests, part of the biodiverse Southern Blue Ridge Ecoregion,[9] early estimates state Helene caused moderate to catastrophic damage to more than 187,000 acres. Nearly 900 miles of Forest Service-managed roads and an estimated 800 miles worth of trails have been damaged.[10]

▶ In Asheville, the largest city in the affected area, eighty percent of homes and businesses were without clean water service for more than seven weeks.[11] During that time, we gathered daily in parking lots to fill jugs with clean water from tanker trucks. Parking lots were also where we took showers and did laundry in purpose-built trailers. For flushing toilets, many toted water from creeks and ponds. Asheville's Mission Hospital, the region's only Level II trauma center, also lost municipal water service. It was without running water for at least four days, getting service eventually by putting into place contingency plans.[12]

▶ Eighty-two public schools were closed for 20 or more days.[13]

▶ Duke Energy, the largest provider of electricity in the area, reported 1.5 million outages in North Carolina. Outages extended for more than a week for nearly 84,000.[14]

▶ More than 70 percent of cell service sites were out of service after the storm, making it impossible for many to call for emergency services.[15]

▶ North Carolina governor Roy Cooper called Helene "the worst storm in our state's history.[16]" His office estimates a $59.6 billion impact, including damage to more than 73,000 homes, 6,900 road and bridge sites, and 44 emergency response facilities.[13] The

President declared Helene a Major Disaster and FEMA designated 39 counties and the Eastern Band of Cherokee Indians for federal disaster assistance.[17] That's an area about the size of Massachusetts.

▶ Across the Southeast, Helene was about 400 miles wide, comparable in size to Hurricane Katrina.[18]

▶ As of late December 2024, the U.S. Army Corps of Engineers had removed more than 700,000 cubic yards of storm debris in western North Carolina. They are contracted to remove 1.5 million cubic yards in total.[19] That's enough debris to fill the Houston Astrodome once, fill the Lincoln Memorial Reflecting Pool 45 times[20], or more than 100,000 dump truck loads.[19] That does not include debris removed by others.

Like many—perhaps most—in the region, my neighbors and I were initially confined to our immediate area by large downed trees, damaged homes, and fallen power lines. Without power, water, cell service, or internet, we were isolated. We didn't know it at the time, but we were the lucky ones.

By the second or third day, someone had figured out that a parking lot at a nearby furniture store had enough of a cell signal to exchange texts, and perhaps a brief voice call. To get there, I held my breath as I drove around tree limbs, under teetering telephone poles, and across what I hoped were dead power lines. I stood in that lot with dozens of others, passing around the few phones lucky enough to draw a weak signal. When I could finally reach my faraway adult children, I tried to sound calm. Still, when I heard their sweet voices, I sobbed.

Until several days later, when we could make our way downtown, we lacked a signal strong enough to see what the rest of the world knew about the storm. And even then, it was hard to look. Instead, information passed mostly by word-of-mouth. For weeks, every morning I plugged a household power strip into my parked electric car and neighbors would gather to enjoy hot coffee ("driveway coffee"), charge their devices, and share what they knew. We learned that many in the area were also isolated in damaged neighborhoods. Others had fared far worse. The Lowe's a few miles away was under water, the shelves of our grocery store were caked with mud, and nearby raging rivers carried away trucks, storage containers, propane tanks, and homes. Every business was closed. Trees breached homes. The hospital's capabilities were limited.

Neighbors grilled up communal "eat-it-before-it-rots" dinners, where we shared more information. One neighbor had an emergency radio and described how she listened live as a man called in to the radio station from his flooded home on nearby Swannanoa River Road. He signed off optimistically, saying "we'll be fine." His body was later found downriver along with those of his wife and grandson, a second grader from our neighborhood elementary school.

Other neighbors told how large sections of beloved area towns had become muddy moonscapes, with homes and businesses destroyed or washed away entirely. Hearing the name of each damaged place felt like a gut punch: Swannanoa, Chimney Rock, Lake Lure, Biltmore Village, the River Arts District, Hot Springs, Marshall. Later we heard about the devastation in Cane Creek in Fairview, Craigtown in Garren Creek, Spruce Pine, and more.

The scale was overwhelming. From the beginning, most people who could help did, and many continue to provide meals, housing, supplies, repair and chainsaw services, a kind shoulder, and more. These efforts are dearly needed to piece our communities back together and are a way for us to gain a small measure of agency over our upended lives.

We've been joined by many helpers from afar, who have come with open hearts and strong arms. Others have donated selflessly to the recovery effort. Unprompted, two experienced members of a FEMA crew remarked to me that the community response here feels markedly selfless—far more so than they're used to seeing. We're enveloped in an almost magical sense of kindness and patience which persists as I write this three months out.

Early on, to try to process the unfathomable, I started to write. It's what I do to help work through strong feelings. I scribbled through tears at my window-lit kitchen table. I'm lucky to be part of the local writers' community, and it occurred to me others might be doing the same thing. Shortly after I got power and internet back—for me, 16 days after the storm—I reached out to talented local writers I knew. That's how this book was born.

I asked them to send me their process-the-storm essays and poems. I then asked local professional artists to do the same. I set a short deadline on purpose—I wanted to capture the creative outpouring from the early throes of realization and recovery. To me, it was important to document this moment.

The work you hold here has been graciously provided without payment to any of the creators. We will donate all profits from book sales to help with the recovery effort.

As the artwork and writing began to populate my inbox, what struck me was the vulnerable nature of the work. That is, these are first-hand accounts of living through the storm, conveyed by those with the talent and training to distill feelings into words and works of art. They share how this place is special—this vibrant land of mountains, streams, creativity, and innovation—and how the destruction wrought by the storm inflicted a profound wound.

It also struck me how the work reflects storm experiences shared by many here from across the region. That is, I had not reached out to people who I knew had suffered dramatic losses. The most harrowing stories have been covered well already—a quick search online will reveal heart-wrenching videos, photos, and articles. Instead, I simply asked people who, in the immediate aftermath of the storm, I thought might feel an urgent need to write or create artwork. I had no knowledge of their individual circumstances.

Even so, everyone who responded had indeed been affected deeply. The loss described in these pages is at once extraordinary and, sadly, so very common here. Those of us who lived through this are now bonded by a collective aura of both trauma and grace.

It's hard to explain to faraway friends and family the impact of this storm. Photographs and videos are shocking, yet don't do it justice. It's like trying to capture the Grand Canyon. It's just too big. What's more, how can you infuse a photo or video of a damaged area with the sting of knowing the beauty of how things used to be? But that's where artists and writers excel, with a drive to convey experiences and emotion in a way that can touch others.

My wish for those who lived through the storm is to find that perhaps this book gives voice to some of their own emotions, and thereby promotes healing. I also hope it will help readers from elsewhere better understand the personal impact of a widespread natural disaster. As I type this, raging fires in Los Angeles fueled by hurricane-force winds have forced my son, along with thousands of others, to evacuate to safety. If mass disasters seem more frequent and more fierce, it's because they are.[21] We know there will be more. Winds and floods devastated our region—this climate refuge hundreds of miles inland. It could happen anywhere. We need to work together to put into place ways to avoid conditions that exacerbate disasters and also to mitigate their effects. Believe me, nobody wants to be in a position to create the work you hold here.

And please know: Here in western North Carolina, we are standing. We are rebuilding. We are eager to welcome visitors again to this magical land we call home.

Thank you.

Shelley McKechnie
Asheville, North Carolina
January 2025

The Second Impossible Thing
Terry Leigh Deal

Impossible tears

wailed across waiting mountain valleys

muddied terrified rivers.

Centuries of limbs snapped like frozen bones.

Five hundred thousand trees were drowned

their sad songs sung downriver.

No one holds on to a wild beauty

this impossible.

Painting the Town
Ann Harris

After it happened I stepped barefoot out onto the upstairs porch and painted my toes. I chose bright orange, the most shocking color, and watched as the sun cusped the edge of the eastern mountains and lit up Mount Pisgah in the distance. It was calm and quiet, even though four massive oak trees had crashed onto our roof. The wind had moved on, and the birds and squirrels were still hiding. Then the sirens started calling out from the fire station a mile away. They wouldn't stop for the rest of the day.

We'd had no power since 3AM, but I knew where all the camping equipment was and had already set up the double propane stove, stationed candles and lighters around the house, and filled the bathtub with water. I'd bought groceries yesterday, and it was warm outside. We'll be fine, I thought, having weathered squalls in the Everglades, typhoons in Asia, and blizzards on Cold Mountain.

I painted my toes, taking the time to first slough off the old polish and file the nails down. I surveyed the way out, wishing I had charged my electric chainsaw as I tallied the many oaks that had fallen across the gravel road even before it turned the corner. Who knew what lay beyond that now, other than a trench my neighbor dug across the road late last night. The trench that kept my older son from getting home after work. My older son who now had no way to reach me by phone, my son who loved photography and probably had gone to shoot what he could see, not realizing Helene would break his home, his family, and the course of his life irreparably.

I painted my toes. By the second coat, MAMA, the Mission Hospital helicopter, was already flying overhead. I wondered whose soul they were trying to save as the pilot flew over the knuckles and ridges of Pisgah, this land of promise. I wondered what they could see, high above me. The bodies of the oaks on the roof dripped and steamed around me as the sun got busy soaking their souls to the sky.

As the polish dried, I looked for the bears, peering into the nooks and hollows where they tended to bed down for the night. It was their typical wake and stretch hour before they made their way across the land on their food circuit before returning at dusk. We knew every boar, sow, and cub, and this was the time of year when a good dozen would graze on acorns in the forest around the house. The cubs, bored of acorns, would break away to snatch ping pong balls from our outside table and roll them around in their mouths like gumballs before chomping them useless and tossing them aside. One of those cubs had become a mom this year and had two cubs of her own that had climbed every oak around the house, curiously peering in our big windows at the two dogs that barked yet ran away. They had everything they needed here, plenty of natural food and water from the spring, shelter from hunters. This ancestral den passed down through the bears like my own nine generations of kin in these hills. I put on my flip-flops and went out to check the extent of the damage.

The oaks covered the right side of the house, heavy and drenched like the spongy lungs of blue whales. They had taken poplars, hickories, and sourwoods down with them. Their branches were entangled, interlocked, as if they had reached out to hold hands as they were uprooted. All around me, in every direction, lay the largest trees of the forest, gasping in shock.

The birds were still silent. The sirens seemed to have taken their voices. I watched as squirrels took tentative steps, looking upward, bewildered, at nothing to climb. The house, the roof overhang sagging a good six feet but holding, seemed the tallest thing standing. To the north along the Blue Ridge Parkway corridor was a solid green wall of trunks and limbs, a good fifteen feet high.

I crawled through the fallen trees like they were rhododendrons. Found the root balls of the giants who had been torn from the saturated ground by the wind. It just didn't make sense. Many of the twin trunks were over three feet in diameter each. These were all the parent trees, some over 100 feet tall, yet they had fallen like dominoes from deep in the national parkland that bordered our property. A twister must have dropped down along the upper ridge, its calamitous path visible ever onward to the north.

To the west, I heard the soft pads and gripping claws of two cubs as they hurtled the downed trunks and soon saw their black noses pushing through a downed holly. I looked for their mama, who tended to bed down with her brood by the shed at night. How in the world would she ever get through? Had she made it, or would I find her soft body, full of milk still yet to be drunk, somewhere under these green masses? Did she know where her babies were? Was she searching for them, as I would search for my eldest, as he would search, too, for a way to find home again?

Circling back to the house, I looked through the downstairs window, checking on my younger son, who was fully covered head to toe by his blanket, blocking out the sun. He had decided to go back to bed since it made sense that he would have the day off school. It made sense to sleep in. He'd already found the solar charger and plugged in his phone, but the typical stream of message notifications that kept his device alive had ceased.

Two hours ago, I had awakened him as the wind rose. Sonorous but hidden by darkness, the storm had swirled quickly in, and he'd stationed himself by the window, eating popcorn in expectation of a good show, his 6-month-old Bernedoodle by his side. Just two hours ago.

I had watched him, my animal body trembling, desperately wanting to keep the experience light for him, but I was wary of the window. I moved him to the center room downstairs, settling the dogs on either side of him on the sleeper sofa, surrounding them with snacks and chocolate milk. He had poured bourbon in my coffee as a joke, and I had smiled.

Then the thuds had begun. Like giant heartbeats, muffled in the thick wind. The trees were falling.

The beats were faint at first, then ever more resonant in surround sound. The ground began to shake, rattling the house. It was like being inside a bass drum kicked repetitively by God.

Dawn rose as the storm intensified, so then we could see the trees bending completely sideways, their branches shaking like frayed scarves from the necks of their trunks. The white oaks, joined by their family root system underground, clasped hands, rising up repetitively together as the gusts berated them. The red oaks, with their shallow root systems, laden with leaves and acorns ready to drop, could not hold. They came undone. As they began hitting the house, I looked at my son, who still, in his disbelief, thought this was fun. My son, whom I could no longer protect. I drank my spiked coffee. I threw the ball for his dog. I wondered where my older son was and enveloped him with the silent runic spells of my ancestors.

My youngest would sleep for hours. Now was the time to find D. How could I make my way out to find him now? I couldn't make it through the gate, which was covered in trees leaning precariously, so I headed east, still on foot, toward the VA hospital. I could hear their generators now, and the sharp stinging sound of sirens continued as they slowly made their way down Tunnel Road.

I looked for a viewpoint, a tree to shimmy up to determine a way less blocked, but there were no trunks with limbs left low enough to climb. The ridgeline had been razed, and whole tops of trees dangled 50 feet in the air. It was a scalping done barehanded rather than with a blade, the heads of the trees cast carelessly aside. I've never seen something more cruel. This pristine forest, a deciduous mecca, had become a wasteland.

I looked at my watch and saw an hour had passed, and I was nowhere near a clear path out. No sounds of traffic were coming from either Maple Springs Road or Bull Mountain. I made my way to where a pile of four trunks had come down, stacking themselves from all four directions, and casting my shoes aside, I climbed up to the highest point I could.

Helene had swept through like a gypsy, exotic and unattached to this land, her heavy skirts swirling as she danced. She had leapt across the valleys, touching down on the ridges, making them her red carpet for the hour. Whatever had caused her squalor, it was clear that she had wanted no one to be more stunning than she.

Long a steward of this land, I pushed through the twisted limbs, laying hands on each downed goliath. Each of these trees had stood tall by me, more than any family I now had. The king and the land are one, I knew. Sobbing in grief, I broke, too. I became unrooted, enraged, unsaved, and insane. Time warped. My voice became a siren and wailed for all that had been severed.

▲ ▲ ▲

Now, two months later, I pick up my son to spend the night at home again for the first time. Both boys had chosen to live with his father across town, where they were far enough away from the river, where their roof was intact, and where they didn't have a view of a wasteland out their bedroom windows. It made sense. Tonight, as I pick him up and drive him home, creeping in disaster-tourist traffic, the winds return. The forecast calls for gusts to 45 miles per hour. By the time we get to East Asheville, the streetlights are out again. Cars lunge across intersections like desperate deer. Trees, many still loosely holding to the ground, bend toward us again. This, his first night home.

Are you ok, I ask him.

The trees are all gone, he remarks, so what's there to worry about?

But I know worry, as mothers do. The roof, damaged and still awaiting repair, could blow clear off. The trees left standing, now dry and cracking from two months of drought, could let loose their limbs, and the house could be lain asunder again.

But our house is strong, I tell him. Remember how the steel beams kept the roof from crashing last time? Remember how the ring of white oaks around the house caught so many other trees, lifting them away from us?

As we crest the hill, the twilight evokes the new wood sheen on the neat stacks of hardwood logs and rows of split wood snaking their way into the forest by the splitter. Two weighty red oaks still lean out and away from the south side of the house, propped up by their resilient white cousins, still waiting to be relieved. I had tucked away the chain saws, canisters of fuel, MREs, and cases of bottled water, hoping to ease my son's return. Tonight, the wind has aborted my plans, and we arrive at a dark home, the power lines severed somewhere by a tree that had waited to fall. I find the headlamps, light the candles. I start the camping stove and make him canned soup and mac and cheese. He retreats to his room to study for the PSAT test tomorrow, and I let him, knowing he will make a perfect score, coveting his ability to make sense out of the nonsensical. I watch out the main room window as our still-resident mama bear leads her two cubs across the gravel driveway to den down for the night. I put my dog, shaking, in the center of my bed, and step barefoot out onto the upstairs deck, pull on my coat, turn on my headlamp. As the wind blows the loose chairs across the wood planks of the deck, I squat, my back against the wall, and paint my toes.

Footprints of Helene
Jaime Byrd

My husband and I live in the Garren Creek community area of Fairview, North Carolina which was one of the hardest hit areas from Hurricane Helene. We had flooding and damage to the entire first level of our home where we continued to be without power, running water, internet, or cell service for 3 weeks. Fortunately, our neighbors and community came together and helped all of us in need.

Our road access out of the area was washed out from flooding and therefore we were stuck for over five days before being able to reach my gallery in the River Arts District, which was another hard-hit area. My newly renovated 2000 square foot art gallery—which I had opened only 8 months before the storm—had catastrophic flooding and destruction. My entire working studio and gallery was flooded with over five and a half feet of water. I lost original art, all my reproductions, tools, art supplies, frames, wood painting panels, furniture, a full kitchen, electronics, photography equipment, and all our office and business gear and supplies. It was devastating.

After the water had receded, the building owner walked into my gallery and spotted two beavers swimming around in the mud and muck. The two critters scurried off before he could capture their presence among the debris and floating artwork. He then noticed one particular painting that was lying flat on a floating easel that had several beaver paw prints in mud all over the piece. I was able to rescue this piece and have it photographed to make into a limited edition giclée reproduction on paper titled, *The Footprints of Helene*.

The beaver is said to be a spirit animal that represents the power of adaptability. They also represent protection and regrowth. I believe this is a strong message for me and for the River Arts District.

This is my first limited edition reproduction that is to help with my gallery and art studio recovery from Helene. To me, this piece of artwork will forever be a sign of remembrance, strength, and growth within our communities, and our creative spirit, as well as a reminder that nature will always win.

When it Comes to You
Brian Railsback

My fine old neighbor has lived for fifty years on Savannah Ridge, a place he simply calls "The Mountain," and he often says we live in paradise, that we are the luckiest people in the world. My wife, Sandy, and I are newcomers—living here for thirty years—and we see The Mountain the same way. Our home sits on three acres, north facing at an altitude of four thousand feet, backed up against a dark forest, with views over a gentle slope that open like a theatre widescreen, miles and miles across the valley to Richland Balsam and the highest point on the Blue Ridge Parkway. Each day the steep wall behind us casts its shadow on the land early; my neighbor, a meticulous retired professor of biology, has never measured a summer temperature over eighty-six degrees here. Ever since we let the land go wild, working on a Certified Wildlife Habitat® designation, spring and summer bring gardens of wildflowers, arranged differently each year. In winter, when it rains at Cullowhee's lower elevation, we often welcome snow. Each season is a gift.

Yet like some people across the world, we notice changes in our little homeland. All the eastern hemlocks on our property expired quickly, as if they suffered heart attacks. One by one, the ash trees have died off as well. The weather has gone from fairly predictable to strangely erratic, like a dependable friend drifting into alcoholism. Summer feels longer, the October dry period continues into November, more rain in December, scant snow or surprising dumps of it in January, February, and March. Spring storms that seem downright enraged, abrupt explosions of roaring wind, unending thunder, jagged strands of lightning. Our wellhouse has been hit twice, water pumps burned out. One April afternoon we saw the top half of a white pine, some seventy years old, rip in half, its top spinning into the air.

After a long dry spell last November, a wildfire blew up in Jackson County and we watched from our deck as it almost topped a ridge nearby. Stunned, we wondered if we should evacuate. The creeping sense that the rules on The Mountain have changed grew on us last May 9, when just after midnight an F2 tornado touched down in our yard. I was awake, watching television, when the pitch of the rain turned into a roar so great—unlike any downpour I've heard before—that it obliterated the sound of trees being blown apart only a football field away. The next morning, Sandy said to me, "something is wrong with the woods across the street."

Like so many people have done after storms in California, Florida, the Philippines, or Bangladesh, we staggered out into the wreckage, our eyes blinking, like children just waking up. The trees that covered the driveway did not just fall; they had been shattered, trunks twisted and rent, the smell of raw tree sap like from some open wound. Two massive pines, broken in half, smashed one of our cars. Speechless and bewildered, we stood in front of a large, ancient apple tree blown to pieces as if hit by a Russian missile. And the ridge across the street, a familiar old forest we took walks in, had been wiped out, a scene from a World War I battlefield. All of this damage occurred in less than five minutes in the dark of night, while we were oblivious.

So we felt a sense of inevitability when we awaited the approach of Helene's remnant on Friday, September 27. We expected the worst, like when The Mountain took a beating from the dregs of Hurricane Opal in October 1995 and four trees fell on our house. With Helene, the power went out, rain pelted, and we noticed the wind first blew from the south and then the north. Some trees fell and our chimney took a hit from a flying branch, cracked open enough to let water into our living room. But the storm surprised us; it was not so bad up on The Mountain, and later we heard that the hurricane's remnant eye passed over us.

Of course, once the power was back on, we learned about the disastrous wind, rain, landslides, and flooding across western North Carolina. Although Cullowhee escaped significant damage, you could feel the wreckage and suffering outside of our valley. "If you know enough about the history of this region, you know that the mountains funnel water into deadly flash flooding," my colleague, Ron Rash, told me a few weeks after the storm. "But I do think this is different. What's happening now is becoming more frequent and we really are in a rough situation."

It's that word, *frequent*, that makes you anxious about the rate of change in our environment and what will happen next. In her monumental book, *The Sixth Extinction*, Elizabeth Kolbert writes of the steep decline of species worldwide; she hopes to convey "the excitement of what's being learned as well as the horror of it." From a scientist's point of view of the amazing rapidity of environmental change caused by human activity, she adds that we are witnessing a "truly extraordinary moment."

These observations are far from comforting.

I used to think that The Mountain, tucked into the deep woods and protected by the folding ridges of the Southern Appalachians, would somehow escape the worst of the world's increasing droughts, fires, floods, and beat-down storms. But Helene shakes that notion, reminds us of the region's great floods of the past and the likelihood we will see stronger and more frequent occurrences in the Anthropocene, the notion of Kolbert and other scientists that we have moved into a human-driven epoch and out of the Holocene that came before it. Once we fully understood what Helene had done, Sandy and I stood on our deck, a little paralyzed by climate anxiety, and we asked, *what happens when it comes to you?* And we wondered, *what do we do?*

Some answers circled above us.

Small airplanes, at first a few and then dozens, were heading to nearby Jackson County Airport. A quick check on social media informed us that with roads washed out or buried in landslides, a large airlift had been organized. Volunteer pilots flew in from states all over, their private planes packed with goods for storm victims in need. Jim Rowell, the airport's manager and a friend I've come to know as a huge supporter of our community, explained to me, "In the eleven-day period, from September 29 to October 9, we had eight hundred and forty operations, thirty-three percent of what the Jackson County Airport would have in an entire year . . . in eleven days. That's four hundred and twenty aircraft in and out." He estimated that three hundred tons of goods were delivered, including food, water, medical supplies, and even toys.

I drove to the airport, noticing all the broken pines, poplars, and oak trees cleared to the side of the roadway, bark and sawdust on the road. I found volunteers near the airport runway, waiting for the next plane to unload. I recognized Western Carolina University students, area business leaders, retirees, church members—it seemed everyone was there. Before a plane rolled in, organizers rounded us up and explained what to do. After it landed, we made a human chain, rapidly moving the packages to a waiting truck. "It was so heartening to see folks from all walks of life rally together and pitch in," Jim said. "Planes came from all directions—North Carolina, Tennessee, South Carolina, Virginia, West Virginia, Kentucky—just everywhere. Our volunteers were mostly local . . . politics and differences were set aside to help our neighbors. This is the America we all want."

When you are out there hustling relief packages, the anxiety eases. Sure, you think of the carbon tax with all those airplanes— there are no easy answers in the 21st century. But here is a massive demonstration of the best of us, the bright side of the collective human soul. Moving boxes, you might think on a wonderful book like Sebastion Junger's *Tribe, On Homecoming and Belonging*, which systematically examines how in crisis human beings naturally protect each other and cohere into a force for good. Junger writes of the "self-determination theory, which holds that human beings need three basic things in order to be content: they need to feel competent at what they do; they need to feel authentic in their lives; and they need to feel connected to others."

And working in line at the Jackson County Airport, we had that. So did all the other people across our mountains, pulling together, from the neighborhood volunteers to the FEMA workers.

The next time the trees on The Mountain bend to the inevitable howling winds, we will welcome the predictable hum of the planes that follow.

Our City is a Body
Kate Krause

Our city is a body,
Curves of the Blue Ridge
Familiar like a faithful lover.

Tendrils of Black Balsam and Chimney Rock
Falling like hair heavy around her waist.
Her beauty, so comforting and stable
That we barely noticed that grounding force.

And we too, are part of that body.
Schools and restaurants and songs of troubadours.
Laughter of children
And bread around tables.

So on that September day
When our veins burst
Floodwaters of Swannanoa, French Broad, and Garren Creek
Thundering like an aneurysm…

We all felt it in our bones, didn't we?
A throbbing from deep in the ground and deep in our bodies…
        crying out for help.

But instead of saying "I hurt," we said, "All of us are dying and we
have to rescue us."

So we rose up.
We tore through the streets and the country roads

With saws in our hands,
Cutting down trees where there once were borders.

We forgot about social hierarchies and political agendas,
And found in each other what we had always been…
Neighbors.

And we all heard it, didn't we?
The rushing of concern
Far and near.
Sirens and confusion,
A limp body on a gurney.

We felt the electric paddles
Against our skin.
Unfamiliar voices yelling "clear."
Shock into the body of our land
And into the bodies of all who inhabit it.

Collective breath in our nostrils
And then, a long darkness.

Like a faithful lover in a hospital bed
It's hard to truly know how much we love something
Until we almost lose it.

But now, can we gather the courage
To open our eyes
And look around?

The ones that love us hold our hands
And massage our temples.
Flowers of every kind

Our City is a Body

Fill the white walls of this recovery room.

A thousand arms hold us.

Adrenaline is still in our sinews
And we are still heaving from the weight of trauma
Knowing the road ahead will be long and arduous.

But…

Our city is a body
With its million systems
Of breweries full of stories
And fiery trees

And neighbors we never knew before
Gathered around a fire.

This ache is too deep for just one person
It is the ache of all of us.

So when you are not strong, I will be strong for you
And when I am not strong, you will be strong for me.

With all of us shakily holding each other up on one side
And our beautiful mountains bolstering us on the other

I truly believe
That together
We will walk into our healing.

The Stormy Clouds of Helene
Cynthia Llanes

I have always loved watching the rain and the foggy mountains from our porch. I painted this scene from our front porch as the apocalyptic storm started brewing above the Pisgah Forest. The wind was so strong it pushed and moved the clouds so fast it became a bit challenging to paint them, but I like painting fast with watercolors because of the nature of the medium. Going with the flow, as they say. Little did I know that these clouds would wreak so much havoc on our beloved Asheville!

Sounds
Anja B. Woody

It's a pleasant fall evening here in the mountains.

21 DAYS

21 days since Helene changed our lives forever.

I went for a walk in my neighborhood. I noticed the sounds. Sounds of the crickets, dry leaves blowing across the pavement, dogs barking. These sounds have now mostly replaced other sounds that became commonplace after Helene. For days and days, there were sounds of helicopters traversing the sky-multiple times a day-from every direction-for days and days. Helicopters, sirens, generators-sounds once rare, now constant.

My thoughts with every siren I heard-what will they find- will they save someone-can they?

Now so many stories, videos and photos of destruction.

EVERYWHERE

Helene has robbed us, robbed us of our quaint small towns. Robbed us of what we once knew. Robbed us of our sense of community, our sense of security.

Hurricanes don't happen here.

Helene filled the rivers, streams, creeks and culverts to more than anyone thought possible. She robbed people of their homes, their belongings and their loved ones.

Large chunks of pavement, trees, trailers, homes and cars tossed around like toys.

I was one of the lucky ones. I sit here in my home that now has power and water-although not drinkable-and I think how incredibly blessed and lucky I am.

But at times, the grief is overwhelming.

When The Waters Turned
Heather West

For 19 years I have answered a deep call to work in this magical place. Officially my title is General Manager of Hot Springs Resort and Spa. However, I simply define my role as being in service to this water. The land and waters of Hot Springs are my soulplace. They connect me to my ancestors, the generators of my family that came before me that walked this same land, touched these same waters. These waters have witnessed my greatest joys and deepest sorrows. These waters have challenged me and mentored me with great sternness and love. However, the lessons I thought I had learned about Hot Springs were only a primer to the final exam that came with Hurricane Helene.

It was Friday morning in Hot Springs, North Carolina, when the sky darkened with the heaviness of a hurricane approaching. Hurricane Helene was making her presence known. The property of Hot Springs Resort and Spa, my workplace for the past 19 years, was oddly quiet. On a typical Friday morning the resort would be bustling with staff getting ready to host guests for a weekend. This morning it was silent. The calm before the storm. I was with a small team of staff members and we were the only people onsite. We were tasked with preparing the 100-acre property for the flood, something we had done before as Hot Springs, a valley along the French Broad River, was prone to minor flooding. The team onsite was a small group tasked with managing the waters in this beloved town, known for its tranquil hot springs and scenic mountain views. We had seen the forecast, had planned for a storm, but nothing could have prepared us for the fury that was about to unfold.

The rain had been steady, the wind howling through the trees, but it was the water that began to rise at alarming speed. As I patrolled the 100-acre property, the land was shrinking and the water was pouring in. Anxiety and fear began to set in, I started to question my choice to be here through this storm, I began to worry about the safety of my team. We were accustomed to the river and its temperamental nature, but this was different. We stood outside, through the thick tree line of the campground we could see the railroad tracks that separated the resort from downtown Hot Springs. The creek that ran through Bridge Street started swelling faster than we could monitor it. At first, it seemed like the water was simply rising along its usual course, creeping over the banks as it had so many times before. But then, something changed.

Without warning, Spring Creek, usually a quiet stream winding through town, backed up at the bridge. The water didn't just flow; it surged. It seemed to rise as if the very earth was forcing it in the opposite direction. In seconds, it began to spill over the road, and what we had thought was manageable became an overwhelming torrent of water. It was as if the town was being attacked by the very thing it had relied on for generations: the water.

The sound was unlike anything I had ever heard; the roar of the floodwaters, the crash of debris, and then, the chilling sound of propane tanks from the downtown businesses hissing as they were carried downstream by the relentless flow. Each hiss was like a warning, a reminder that this was no longer just a storm—it was a force of nature that we couldn't control.

In those moments, fear set in. We were still trying to assess the situation, but when the water began creeping across the railroad tracks, it was clear we were losing control. Time began to move as quickly as the water. Somehow the morning had become early afternoon. Swiftwater rescue teams arrived to help people out of buildings that were quickly taking on water, sirens cutting through the chaos, their presence a reminder of just how dangerous the situation had become. As anxiety was quickly becoming reality, I made the call to leave. I found my team in the campground and told them we had to leave, now! Personal safety was now paramount to saving assets. There was no point in trying to stand our ground against a flood this powerful.

We packed up as quickly as we could, watching helplessly as the town we loved was overtaken by the floodwaters. Water was pouring over the railroad tracks from Spring Creek and the French Broad was furiously swelling. It was a heartbreaking departure. The rushing water, which had brought life and healing to the town for so long, was now the destroyer.

I didn't sleep much that night, and when I returned on Saturday, the scene that greeted me was nothing short of apocalyptic. The small, picturesque town of Hot Springs, the very place where people came to heal and find peace, was unrecognizable. The resort, once bustling with visitors, was reduced to a pile of debris. The streets, now filled with silt and remnants of homes and businesses, spoke of the devastation that had unfolded in such a short span of time.

The water that had been a symbol of calm and renewal had turned on us in an instant, showing just how fragile our relationship with nature can be. As a self-proclaimed steward of this land and water I felt that I had worked so hard to protect it, to keep the balance, but in the end, I was reminded of how small I am in the face of such power. The loss was unimaginable. Not just of the physical town, but of the heart of the community, the life that had flowed through this place for so many years.

The scars from the storm are deep but Hot Spring will rebuild. The water we loved, the water we worked to preserve, had thrown a grand fit, and in the end, it was us who had to bear the cost.

Dispatch
Shelley McKechnie

I chose my house in Asheville, in large measure, because of the giant weeping cherry tree out front. It's taller than the house, standing sentinel over the pond fifty-one steps below. Over the years I've rebuilt maybe half those steps myself, the ones where the rain would pool atop sunken stone pieces. You can tell which ones I fixed first, as they're kind of uneven.

Each April, the tree's wispy hanging branches explode in pink blossoms. I'm not sure why the intensity of the display always surprises me, but it does. By May, the blossoms give way to new green leaves. That's when I know to hang a feeder from the eave of my front porch roof, waiting for the hummingbirds to take up warm-weather residence in the tree. I'd like to think it's the same pair that returns every year. Sometimes they have babies. This year it's just been the two of them.

I've taken to sipping hot tea in the mornings as I lean against the porch railing and watch them flit around the feeder. They jockey for position, like a pair of little fighter jets, in impossibly choreographed arcs. Every few moments, one alights on the feeder's perch just long enough to take a quick sip through a fake red flower. It jumps away quickly, lingering no more than an instant, as if the perch were electrified. I stand there, right there, as still as I can. I'm close enough to think maybe I'm feeling the breeze from wings beating too fast to see. The birds don't seem to mind me standing so close.

A few times a week, when I look out my oversized front windows towards the tree, I see black bears amble by on their way to the adjacent woods. They lumber along, sometimes flipping over rocks to look for bugs, sometimes casting a disinterested glance my way. Once at dusk I went out to the yard to spray a nest of ground bees or wasps or whatever nasty swarm that had attacked me when I was mowing the lawn. When I got to the nest, I noticed a big paw had already scraped it out for me. Problem solved. That marked the start of an easy truce between us.

One morning this past September, alone in the house, I woke to the sound of wind and rain. It had been raining hard for days. The power had been out since the night before. I ran one hand along the back of my family room couch, past the smiling pictures of my family on the adjacent table, as I made my way to open the blinds. I had expected the wind and rain would intensify with the arrival of tropical storm Helene. But when I looked out the window, straining to discern shapes through the dawning sky, I saw sheer violence. High winds hurled big handfuls of debris sideways, flying past too quickly to tell what they were made of. Reflexively I took a few steps back away from the window. My jaw dropped open, the way you see in cartoons. I blinked hard, but the scene didn't change. The weeping cherry boomeranged back and forth, its thin branches whipping in faint silhouette against the gray eastern sky. Thick branches from taller trees snapped off and dropped like bombs onto the rhododendrons and azaleas.

My phone screeched in my pocket. I picked it up to see an evacuation alert text. A nearby dam was at risk of failing, it said. Go now to a designated shelter. But the shelter was miles away across town. In this howling storm, I didn't think I could make it. I texted a neighbor a few blocks over, who replied that she had had power until moments before. She had seen on TV that the order was for people closer to the rivers – the French Broad and the Swannanoa. She reminded me that our homes were at a relatively high elevation. So I decided to stay put, for the moment anyway. I feared for neighbors on lower ground.

Through the pounding rain, I couldn't see the neighbor's house across the street, or my pond. The storm culvert feeding the pond must have turned into a giant firehose, I thought. Were the fat koi flailing helplessly? Were muddy currents hurling the orange goldfish over the pond's edge into Haw Creek? Was the dock—with its crisp white benches—still there?

I ran to the other side of the house, to a window facing the rising mountainside beyond my back deck. A forest of towering oaks, birches and trees whose names I don't yet know still held onto their green leaves, a few weeks too early to change colors. I looked up to see them holding tight and flapping like stiff little flags in unison as the wind and rain wailed like a jet engine.

The sheer volume of rain triggered thoughts of flooding. I hurried to the attached garage to check the driveway, where rainwater would sometimes pool a bit. Forgetting the power was out, I mashed the button on the wall to open the garage door. Of course nothing happened. So I jumped up to yank free the emergency door release, then hoisted open the door from the bottom, in one quick clean-and-jerk motion. My strength surprised me, as I heard the heavy door slam up against the end of the ceiling tracks. To my shock, I saw a torrent of water streaming down the driveway towards me. Roilng eddies churned inches away from where I stood in the garage doorway, far closer than I had ever seen. The water was rising fast. The driveway drainage grate must be clogged with leaves, I thought. I reached for an outdoor broom, trying to decide, stupidly, if it was worth it to run out and clear the drain. As if that would have made any difference. As if a fat broom in my thin arms was any protection from this Noah's Ark of a storm.

▲ ▲ ▲

You get a warning when a big tree is about to fall. There's a distinct sound, a series of cracking noises, like when you break a handful of too-long spaghetti before putting it in the pot. Somehow, the cracking is far louder even than the wind. I had heard it once in a storm years ago, and forever after it's easy to recognize. It's the same way anyone my age can recall with utter clarity, say, the sound of a dial-up modem connecting.

If you listen closely—and of course you would—you can hear individual roots crack free. Then there's a pause when the cracking stops. The pause lasts a second or two, give or take. You don't even hear the wind anymore, even though it certainly still roars. The pause is long enough to consider if the rafters above you might be able to hold back a big tree. It's long enough to consider diving under the car. It's long enough to consider that running might put you in harm's way. It's long enough to wonder if you can judge the size and speed of the tree by the length of the pause, the way you might mark time between lightning and thunder. It's long enough to realize that a tree is on its way down, somewhere close.

▲ ▲ ▲

As I stood frozen in my garage, gripping the useless broom, I focused all my energy on listening. I hoped the next sound would be the thud of the tree hitting the ground. But it wasn't. Instead it was a single loud crack, louder than the wind, louder than a gunshot, louder than the heartbeat inside my ears. Wood-on-wood. Did I jump? Did I scream? I don't remember. I dropped the broom and bolted inside, past places and things that, one-by-one, surprised me by how normal they looked—the washer and dryer, the kitchen, the family room.

Normal ended when I got to the back corner guest bedroom. Rainwater was gushing down through the ceiling fanlight onto the bed. A couple feet over, along a line where ceiling drywall panels meet, a waterfall cascaded onto the carpet. Growing water stains along the tops of the walls telegraphed where water was running down behind walls. Thank goodness, though, there was no tree inside the house. There was no daylight where it shouldn't be.

Out the two windows, instead of seeing my red wooden deck, all I could see was a thick tangle of branches and leaves – the lower part of the trees that had pierced the roof above me. The walls and windows had held.

I quickly packed a go bag—a change of clothes, a water bottle, a can of tuna—and threw it by the door. I wasn't sure the damaged house could withstand the wind much longer. I needed to know when the storm might stop. The internet had gone out with the power the night before, so I pulled out a chair at my kitchen table and sat to phone my faraway adult daughter. It should ease up in fifteen minutes, she said, then it should taper off. That was blissfully precise but also seemed like a long time. Stay out of the attic, don't fix the leaks now, don't put out buckets yet, and go to the basement, she said. I promised, and I did. I was grateful for her clear thinking.

Once the worst of the wind was over, and the rain had mostly stopped, I walked outside, carefully dodging fallen tree limbs and trunks across my driveway and the street. I met up with neighbors who were also out checking on each other. Although there was damage, everyone on the street was okay. I went back and surveyed the huge mass of trees on my roof and saw where they had broken through. I found wood scraps in my basement, and a tall neighbor climbed with me into the attic and together we patched the holes from the inside. By then, we realized nobody had cell service, internet, or water. Trees and downed power lines blocked the roads. We couldn't leave, we couldn't contact anyone, and nobody could get to us. We were on our own.

The next morning the sun was out. I remained in ignorance of both the utter devastation beyond and the outpouring of love that would follow. I was standing on my front porch when I heard the buzz of a single hummingbird. It flew towards me from deep inside the branches of the intact weeping cherry. Instead of its usual flitting around, it landed on the feeder and sat, just sat, for a full five minutes.

Helene
(True Love Endures Everything)
Chrys Corn Goodman

During the hurricane I sat looking out at the wind blowing horizontally across the trees in my yard like a freight train at full speed. I listened to the sound of the wind screaming and rattling hard through my old, old windows, trees breaking and falling, and metal roof tins flapping like flags and banging on the barn outside. Power was out. Cell service was out. Radio was out. No news or outside contact except what I could see out my door. Because we live on a hill and our road was blocked by fallen trees, I had no idea of the flooding and devastation that was happening around my city, so I went upstairs to my studio and painted. She showed up, looking like she's about to throw blows. I named her Helene.

Before Helene
Jenny Lee and Debbie DeWall

Before the rains came
Before you got back from the golf tournament
Before it started raining at rehearsal
Before the play was postponed
Before the wind blew
Before the power went out

Before the mountains could no longer protect you
Before you went to stay with friends
Before you couldn't get a hotel room
Before you hoped you didn't overstay your welcome
Before the silence was loud
Before the buzzing of the chainsaws

Before the hum of the generators filled the silence
Before the whirring of the helicopter blades
Before telephone poles snapped in half
Before you watched football using your hotspot
Before you lost cell service
Before the people could leave their homes

Before you lost the freedom to do what you used to do
Before mud swallowed your yard
Before that house on the hill broke in half
Before that other house filled with mud
Before the trees fell on your garage
Before your life was fractured

Before the schools closed indefinitely
Before you got three feet of rain in two days
Before the rivers crested two feet above flood level
Before you were mandatory evacuated to Ingles
Before the rain and the thawed food mingled in a puddle below your feet
Before you got news

Before you walked back to your neighborhood in the rain
Before your neighbors had a cookout
Before the candles were lit
Before the food went bad
Before you drove around and saw total devastation
Before mud frosted parking lots

Before the bridges washed out
Before the roads broke apart
Before you saw trees on top of homes
Before sinkholes swallowed buildings
Before I40E slid down the mountain
Before I40W became a river

Before you saw the tangled power lines
Before you were trapped in your town
Before you were horrified by the damage
Before pets lost their people
Before Ice water was a luxury item
Before cars floated down the French Broad River

Before Chimney Rock fell
Before Lake Lure swallowed the remains of Chimney Rock
Before floods swept the River Arts District away
Before Biltmore Village was ruined

Before Helene

Before businesses were closed forever
Before so many became homeless

Before the shelters were full
Before emergency rooms were full
Before the landslide began
Before the water ran out
Before the sewers backed up
Before disinformation flooded social media

Before the neighbors shared their generator
Before the mail stopped
Before trash pick up stopped
Before your neighbors dug out the road
Before the Cajun Navy brought Starlink
Before main streets had rapids

Before routine medical care became critical
Before you couldn't get groceries
Before you saw families searching for loved ones
Before the scared children cried
Before you had to boil water without power
Before the bodies piled up

Before the ghosts became real
Before you put updates on Facebook
Before you worried about people you didn't know
Before the damage was assessed
Before the trees were cut down
Before the linemen came

Before FEMA arrived
Before the National Guard flew in

Before the clean up began
Before trees became piles of logs stacked in yards
Before you lost track of the days
Before you could only pay in cash

Before you put $500 in your bra
Before the grocery store shelves were empty
Before you waited three hours to get gas
Before you went to food lines
Before your friends and family checked in
Before people understood the damage

Before you were in shock
Before the adrenaline left your brain
Before the truth came out
Before your brother went to the ICU

Before Helene.

Heart of an Artist
Raphaella Vaisseau

All my life, I've marched forward - overcoming obstacles, learning from experiences, and believing I was progressing on my spiritual path of greater expression of the Light within and the ministry of my heart through my work in the world. I'm single and in my later years at seventy-seven. I've been happily living my dream of being a self-supporting artist for almost three decades.

The destruction of my life's work in the flood waters of Hurricane Helene in a single day shook me to the core. It's not just the heartbreaking loss of my artwork and my primary source of income. It's the loss of community, the loss of a space to share my heart through my artistic expression, the loss of a destination for art lovers to come to commune with me and the other artists here. It's the loss of what I thought I was living, what I believed about the world and my place in it, and the uncertainty of beginning again.

I believe healing will take some time personally, and for our entire community. Cycles of grief continue as I am increasingly aware of how fragile I am. Days after the storm, I felt the strength of a phoenix within me, pushing me to survive and embrace new beginnings, unsure of what that may look like. In the beginning, I tried to hold the vision of looking back to this time from two years from now and telling the story of how I survived and the silver linings that came from it. Gradually, determination gave way to acceptance of the enormity of what recovery would require. Emotions erupt suddenly, and tears flow as I repeatedly touch to the depth of my grief. I acknowledge it's hard to be alone, it's harder after sundown, and it's harder at my age. Yet, I allow myself to process this grief with patience, love, and self-care.

I meditate and hear words from Spirit whisper to me, "It's not your fault. All is well. You will survive this too, like the other times you tell stories of. Breathe, my love. All is well."

High Winds and Rising Waters
Wayne Erbsen

I never thought it could happen here. Not in my hometown, anyway. Over the almost fifty years I've lived here I've weathered more than a few major storms, but nothing like I recently experienced with horrible Hurricane Helene. Of course, I have always heard of hurricanes in Florida and in the Gulf states. But in the mountains of North Carolina? Never.

On Wednesday, September 25, 2024, the rain was coming down hard all day, as hard as any rain I can remember. But it came as a complete shock when I woke up the next morning to have no electricity in my apartment, though I still had running water. It wasn't until the following day that the wind really picked up. I found out later that where I'm living in Arden, North Carolina, the winds were running about 50 mph with wind gusts even higher. When I looked out my bedroom window that morning, I could see and feel the heavy rainstorm pounding my windows. Peering out, I could make out the root balls of multiple trees down in the woods which were blown over by the fierce winds that were still raging. It felt that at any minute, a tree could come crashing through my window.

When I tried turning on my computer in my dark room, I realized that it was running on its battery. Turning to CNN news, I started to grasp the gravity and enormity of the destruction in the wake of hurricane Helene. News reports revealed that the entire Asheville area was the scene of horrific widespread destruction. Uprooted trees were everywhere. Power and water lines were down. Cars turned upside-down. Muddy water was up to the second story of many homes and businesses. Some of the most ravaged areas were in Swannanoa, Black Mountain and neighboring towns like Marshall or Lake Lure, North Carolina. These places were literally ripped out by their roots.

To me, these towns weren't just random names on a map but were some of my favorite places that were now gutted and left for dead. Places like Swannanoa, where I lived for eight years, were ravaged. Could it be that my old farmhouse in Swannanoa was still standing? Or had it been washed away by Bee Tree Creek, which was just across the road?

I soon found out that Marshall, North Carolina was completely swamped when rising waters of the French Broad River jumped its banks. In fact, the Old Depot, one of my favorite places to perform with the student band that I coach at the University of North Carolina at Asheville, was completely gone, with nary a trace that it ever existed.

Logging on to Facebook, I came upon a video of a house in Marshall, North Carolina of a friend of mine being washed away by the raging waters brought on by torrential rains that turned low areas into swamps. Her house was ripped off its foundation and torn to pieces. How sad, because I knew that her house had been home to her musical family for several generations. Her father was also a friend of mine and was a famed local fiddler. Her brother was a great banjo player. Helene was surely hitting me hard. I replayed the video several times to hammer home that the scenes of destruction that I was seeing on my computer screen were real and that many people that meant a lot to me were hurting. I started to realize that I was one of the lucky ones who was only suffering mild inconvenience compared to the tragic life-changing scenes of destruction everywhere.

I then frantically tried getting in touch with my two daughters who lived with their families in the Asheville area. My phone calls and emails weren't going through, but I was relieved to soon connect with both of them via texts. At Annie's house in east Asheville, a ginormous red oak tree had come crashing down in the wee hours of the morning. Luckily, it narrowly missed her house, but some of the massive limbs did some damage to the roof of her porch. The root ball was over twenty feet tall with part of it landing on top of her car. Of course, Annie had lost power and water.

My other daughter Rita fared a little better. The home she shares with her husband and their baby was somehow spared but a limb of a giant oak tree in their backyard hung perilously over the roof of their house. They lost power and water as well. Because of the danger that dangling limb posed, Rita knew that they would be in danger if they stayed there. Luckily, her sister Annie welcomed her to stay at her Airbnb that wasn't being used, so Rita and her family moved over there temporarily.

It was several days before I even thought of daring to leave the relative safety of my retirement community. When I did, I didn't get far because of the many downed trees and power lines that littered the road in both directions. It was a strange feeling that I couldn't really drive anywhere. Best to stay put for now.

Reflecting on the wide range of destruction caused by hurricane Helene, I knew that this catastrophe would change Asheville and its people forever. I feel so bad for all those who lost their homes, businesses, and family members. It's going to be a long road back to anything like life as normal in the Asheville area.

As a bluegrass musician, I often process life through my ears, so it was natural for me to think of a song about fearsome rains and rising waters. My thoughts quickly turned to a true song that Carter Stanley of the Stanley Brothers wrote entitled "The Flood," which was about a catastrophic flood of 1957 that struck a fierce blow to eastern Tennessee and eastern Kentucky. The next time I get out my guitar and sing it, the words will resonate and make me think of Hurricane Helene, which hit western North Carolina even harder than the fabled flood of 57.

My Palette Before and After

Gail S. Drozd

Remnants #4

Prior to Hurricane Helene, I painted with vibrant oil pigments. I enjoyed the challenge of capturing nature in its many forms. Little did

I know what an unexpected place nature would take me, literally and creatively.

When Hurricane Helene struck, my husband and I fared better than many. But for days the outside world slowly slipped away from our fingers. We had no idea of the damage to the surrounding Asheville area. Out-of-state friends texted accounts of deaths and areas that had been washed away. It was hard to take in…first photo image was of the town of Chimney Rock. Unbelievable. We had taken our granddaughter there in the spring to the Gem Mine, now gone. Swannanoa, gone. Our favorite haunts: White Duck Taco, gone, Tobacco Barn, gone, River Arts District and the Marquee, a hip art gallery where I displayed my oil paintings for over two years, gone—all suddenly swept away.

On Day 12 after the storm, I received an email from the Marquee, requesting help to recover any art or goods that were salvageable. Whatever time or energy one had to help was appreciated. Despite the concern about the toxicity of the air and mud my husband and I wanted to help. While driving south on Riverside Dr. heading to the River Arts District, we met the destruction head-on—mud, debris, plastic wound around trees, metal, deserted vehicles, garbage, signage, wires, wood, cement slabs stripped of their landmark buildings making it hard to recall what had been there—the lonely foundations patiently waiting, a weird sort of clean slate. Clean-up crews, dump trucks, bulldozers, signal men; along with upended train tracks and an oddly beautiful blue sky without a cloud.

Mother Nature can be cruel. Yet in my mind, I began to see possibility.

We approached the Marquee: a simple structure, cinder block walls with a metal roof. It's a huge, 50,000 square-foot space that hosted over 300 artists and vendors. We entered the blown-out doorway from the south, the furthest side from the French Broad River. All was quiet, solemn, the normally vibrant beat of the music that would permeate the building was missing. We walked slowly through the varying depths of mud and muck that lay on the cement floor, textured with footprints and shards of objects that were left behind. It took some time to adjust to the darkness.

It seemed fruitless to even be there, and we kept asking ourselves, why did we come? Then we found a piece of pottery in the slime and set it near the outside wall, and then another object—bits of beauty, sadly stained now. There was a huge pile of debris at the north end of the building, the main entrance. Interesting. The water must have entered from the south and pushed everything to the other end. Displays, wood, art and materials of all sorts were piled high, Jenga-like. The Marquee signature umbrellas were still hanging from the ceiling, perhaps 18 feet up. Amazing.

As we looked at the pile, there was an abstract blue, black and white painting teetering 12 feet on top...my friend's painting? We couldn't tell from where we were. But just then she and her husband arrived. I asked if she thought it was hers? She did, we were all excited...grabbing a long one-by-four, I gently coaxed the mystery piece down and sure enough it was hers! Crazy, how it survived 15 feet of water, warped yet salvageable.

In that moment, I felt hope and excitement for her to have her painting back—this survivor. Perhaps that is why we were picking through the goo...to restore a little joy to an artist...to reunite her with a creation that had survived the unbeautiful side of nature.

I had four paintings that were lost; but that all paled to what others lost. Still, I had no expectations of ever having them back. I returned to the Marquee several times to help the overall search. I took many photos with my phone during this time. There was something lonely about the objects left behind. Yet beautiful in that they survived. They had a new story to tell.

Some days later, I got a text from a fellow artist saying she found one of my smaller paintings! What? No? Really? Amazing! Then . . . another text that another smaller painting survived. Unbelievable!

When I got them, they were caked with mud but surprisingly un-scathed when I hosed them off. What would they say if they could talk?

My artistic outlook changed that day. Seeing first-hand the power of Hurricane Helene, this unnatural disaster, I was inspired to create a new body of work. Not the vibrant oil landscapes this time but mixed media pieces. I wasn't sure of my direction but let my intuition and desire lead. The underpinning of this work would be my lonely, heartbreaking photographs on a wood panel. That in place, I experimented with acrylic paint and different mediums to create the Marquee mud effect–encasing twigs, sticks, grasses and mulch with thick paint, and securing orphan objects I found along the way. This artistic flotsam was the look and feel I wanted to share.

A closer look at my work reveals small surprises, like how some of the grass blades are green–small symbols of the rebirth that my heart tells me is coming soon. In that spirit, I have titled my new body of work: *"Remnants."*

27 Days Away

Brian Longacre

Nature belittles us

Her storms humiliate

Send us shivering into bathtubs

and doorways, into shelters and rooms like wombs

Unblinking and breathless, crying

But today, now 27 days since the flood, I sit "safe" on a bench beside the river

The sky is swept blue, the autumn air crisp with 52°, and the river slides by in quiet time

And this, too, humiliates

This pristine beauty too belittles us, belies

We who pined life, worried that we might die in waves of thicked water that rose and rolled, thicked with grandfathered farms and furniture and family, thicked with every known thing racing on a river hellbent to beat the breath out of all,

But this river, today, whose water is 27 days away, where once I craved to sit beside her, to listen as I lingered, now I stare at her and squint, reminded that I am small and she, a whore.

Quest for the Hurricane Playbook:
An Uncaffeinated Account
Elizabeth Schulte Roth

It is early Wednesday evening and the rain has been pounding on my windshield for about an hour, which is about as long as I have been talking my friend off the ledge through her impending divorce. Offering advice-while-driving is my favorite pastime. Got a problem? I've got the podcast that can solve it. I pass the entrance gate to the Biltmore Estate and move into the center of the two lanes to avoid the water that is filling up and covering the sides of the street. The sky has faded to black long before it should and I'm afraid if I actually make it to my writing class, the road will be flooded when it's time to drive home.

I turn around and go with my gut, something I am trying to do these days but must defend. I am a rule follower, and ditching class for weather is not in my playbook. I feel guilty when I send my teacher an email that night to apologize for my absence. "Blaming the weather" is a very foreign phrase for me.

The following day's news is filled with photos of flooding in Biltmore Village and hints of an impending storm called Helene. My friends are emptying their boutiques and placing sandbags in front of their doors. I text to offer help and one responds that she should be fine because the rain has stopped, falsely assuming that this storm had passed through yesterday. A real estate colleague says that she is booking showings for the afternoon in case of morning rain. When my hairdresser texts her clients to reschedule in case of bad weather, one responds that the Weather Channel predicts *only* 30 to 35 mile-an-hour winds during her appointment so no need to cancel.

Born and raised in South Florida, I snicker at the alarm as I grew up around hurricanes. In sixth grade, I cried for days because Hurricane David postponed my first day of school and delayed my nine-year plight to strap and click that bright orange school patrol belt onto my uniform, my quest for keeping the rules overshadowed by the title of "super dork" now earned for the foreseeable future.

One of the many reasons we relocated to my husband's Asheville hometown in 2012 was the climate protection we craved. It's a bit ironic that our moving day temperature of 100 degrees is still the hottest on record. Now he is at a conference in Dallas and our teenager is away at boarding school, so I am relishing my empty-nester status with our fox terrier Tracy until 7:12 am on Friday when the oven beeps to alert the loss of electricity. No power means no coffee and the last text before I lose cell service is a cancellation of a meeting that morning, the person fearing that the weather may be an "issue". I am so unprepared that the only candles that light up my home are scented and gifted, wafting the sweet smell of an overcompensating spa director.

I stumble out to the living room while Tracy hides under the bed, the rain pummeling the gutters with a series of gong-like bangs. The trees are swaying from side to side, with a "Weeble Wobble but they don't fall down" kind of cadence. Sheltered by our covered porch, a squirrel is perched outside on the couch pillow, hiding under the ceiling fan to take advantage of a few dry minutes. Instead of running or being chased or barked at like usual, it's rubbing its ears, shaking and scratching off the drops of water from its fur while fighting with the wind to keep steady.

There is one tree that worries me, because its twin fell a few years ago during a violent storm. Our then six-year-old was sitting in this very same spot on the couch when we heard a thunderous crash. I noticed the tree had fallen into the historic graveyard that sits just between our yard and our neighbor's home, smashing the fence but protecting the headstones of those buried there. Our community's developer is sworn to protect it so we don't have a *Poltergeist* situation, although we did tell our child that it was a tree farm until they turned thirteen and begged to have a Halloween party there.

When the tree guy arrived to clean up the debris, he said the tree was not supposed to fall that way. He pointed to the distended and curled roots, noting that the weakened side coupled with the soft soil would indicate that it should have crushed right through our house, specifically the exact spot where our child was sitting that day.

As this twin tree sways, I pray that those same guardian angels kick in again while distracting myself with Miranda July's latest book *All Fours*. Not sure if this much-talked-about menopausal romp is appropriate reading material and I feel guilty that I'm not enjoying it more. The book that everyone is gushing about is totally not working for me.

There is a break in the storm and Tracy needs to pee, so I walk out the front door and in the middle of the street, cowering from hanging trees and limbs cluttered on the ground. I am curious and still uncaffeinated. A trip to the Starbucks sounds like a good plan, until I realize that the unpowered garage door could keep me stranded. Pulling up the handle only offers a few inches of space, so I grab a ladder and grunt my best power-bitch growl until it finally lifts up enough to get momentum to go all the way. Driving down our block, I dodge and weave through the fallen debris for the mile it takes to get to coffee. But the streetlights are all out, swinging from the wires and teasing my ignorance, the only things missing are the tumbleweeds bouncing down the road to the twangy country guitar soundtrack. I pull into an empty parking lot outside of a BP gas station and see that I have one bar of cell service to tell my husband I'm ok. One by one the cars start to pull in, each driver gets out and walks to pull open the store's door only to realize it's closed. This continues for about ten minutes—car parks, driver gets out and walks to door, pulls without success, shakes head and returns to car—until I can't help myself. I roll down the window and alert each one that it's closed before they stop the engine, dashing dreams one by one.

I drive a few blocks until I have to brake hard to avoid the pile of trees in the road. I turn around by the Dunkin' Donuts (still no coffee) and get about five feet before an electric pole and sparking wires send me the other direction. This is the first of many times I will describe this new reality as "apocalyptic". Although my family calls me "The Catastrophizer"—able to predict a worst-case scenario and spot the nearest exit at superhero speed—I can't seem to find the escape route now. My stomach roils with uncertainty, the uncaffein- ated head aches with this new and most uncomfortable situation. What are the rules when there are no rules?

The neighborhood is now filled with men clutching their chain- saws, crawling from block to block to make some sort of path through the chaos. One of my neighbors will need someone with a crane to dislodge the tree pierced into her roof. Her husband is also out of town and she tells me that if we still don't have electricity to- morrow morning, she's hooking up her coffee machine to the car battery. Clusters of people gather in whatever clear spot of street they find, sharing information and offering assistance. Some meet for the first time, but shake hands and hug each other like long lost loves.

A few years ago, I met my neighbor Gabriela because she was walking her dogs while speaking Spanish into the phone and we bonded over our Miami roots. Now she is knocking at my door to in- vite me to Shabbat dinner. She knows that although I was raised a Catholic, I consider myself Jewish-adjacent as an every-Saturday-in- middle school Bar/Bat Mitzvah attendee. Her husband has expertly grilled their freezer-finds and as they light the candle, my shiksa heart bursts with gratitude.

On Saturday Tracy and I are up early to scout out a possible cof- fee shop only to join a line of cars snaked outside an Ingles grocery store. Pulling up to the pained faces of employees desperate to help, the window is just halfway down when they throw scores of bakery items into the front seat and open the back door to donate a bag of ice. Moms who usually balk at store-bought, sugary cinnamon rolls now hug to thank me when I deliver the sweets and news that the nearest gas pump could open soon. We hear hard-to-believe stories including a neighbor's mother-in-law in Biltmore Forest who miraculously left her bed for the bathroom at four am on Friday at the exact time the tree fell onto her pillow, scratching her husband badly but both surviving. A neighbor I've never met compliments Tracy and then offers me her instant coffee that she makes on the gas grill. My caffeine withdrawal must be showing.

Walking miles uphill to find a bar of cell service is the new workout. Later that afternoon, my neighbor passes me on the way down, remarking that I must have already maxxed out my daily steps. My confident stride is a ruse, however, as this current situation is a problem I cannot solve with a podcast.

There is still a case of fancy French wine that I bought at a country club dinner last summer hidden in the coat closet, and I keep racing by its door to ignore it. What used to offer me solace—sitting on my porch with a glass or three of wine—has changed as I have just celebrated a year of sobriety. Instead I grab the melted peppermint ice cream from the cooler, spoon it like soup and call it dinner.

On Sunday morning I hear that the Hilton in Biltmore Park might have coffee so I park across the street and see what I can find. It is there that I meet the Man of Doom. After the usual pleasantries, he breaks into a rant about the water system. It's kaput, out for weeks at least, and people are getting restless and angry. I feel trapped with out a plan, gas, or my family, sweating as I race back to my car. I'm frustrated that I can't get beyond our neighborhood to help while also feeling incredibly helpless like I should be better at this. My mother-bear instincts have been declawed, and I'm scraping for any bits of guidance.

Finally my husband lands in Charlotte and commandeers a rental car as well as the last bag of ice at the Quik Trip gas station on I-26 which has just reopened to traffic. He's secured a cold-brew concentrate and with a nod to my now-abandoned playbook, I ignore the directions to add water and gulp it down without any guilt.

On Monday we find gas and a way out to South Carolina to stay with my niece. We arrive to see CNN Breaking News on the television and for the first time I see the devastating pictures that show the world a region's horrific demise. To us, however, it details the destruction of our friends' businesses, our favorite coffee shops demolished, and our go-to restaurants underwater. Each video portrays what we think of as a disaster, but one that usually happens to others who live far away. There is no playbook for this, no rules to follow and too many problems to solve. A post-disaster etiquette now includes greeting our neighbors with an authentic ask of how they are doing. We slow down behind rescue trucks, wag our fingers at those who dare to honk. We find volunteer shifts, sharing fundraising opportunities and the never-ending search for patience in every corner of our beloved Asheville.

Breaching Limits
Kimberly Smith

Breaching Limits helped me work through cascading emotions as I viewed the devastation brought by the hurricane. Debris from the River Arts District (actual debris used) shows how the river breached its limits and left remains hanging. The sound of military helicopters was constant.

The support, volunteers, and rescue teams on the ground surrounded our senses. Our community was propelled into action in ways that break all limits and barriers. We were carried by a strong FEMA and Army Corps of Engineer presence, by our first responders, and through the responses of charities and churches. Barriers to access, prejudices, and endless tasks are moving aside. Watching Asheville rebound continues to be astounding. *Breaching Limits* is one in a series inspired by the storm.

Hurricane Helene or: How I Learned to Stop Worrying and Love the Void

M.B. Holloway

Boy howdy! Are these troubled times unfolding in distraught spaces or what? Tossed by existential uncertainty; casting about for a lifeline of apprehension; something to guide us back to the calm harbor of Pre-Helene normalcy. But the storm's dread-fog lingers; concealing the port's entrance; obscuring comprehension about this Post-H. world. Though parched for meaning, we mustn't drink the storm's foul waters lest we become sick with ignorance and fear.

Are we damned to drift directionless through the haze of an indefinable life-after-the-storm? Talk about soul crushing levels of disease. Must it be so bleak? Does not this opacity, of necessity, contain its antithesis? A clear-eyed phoenix shed of tragedy; hatched in spite of—and because of—the storm's erasure of all lived-and-historical understanding; waiting for us to coax it from the murky abyss so it may sing of renewed truth. Surely, a kernel of some such to-emerge-truth could have lodged itself under a rock and there weathered the violence wrought by that colorless, transparent, and tasteless liquid; held fast while future was washed away, earth was torn asunder, and memory was buried. If this new understanding exists, it's languishing beneath Helene's backwash. And if we could somehow define the storm—map its contours—we could navigate its detritus, shovel out the muck, and claim this treasure.

Well, what is Helene? More than a meteorological phenomenon for sure; winds have calmed, and waters receded, but H.H. has not left. What is it that stayed behind? Like anyone with such a mystifying question, I asked the godhead-internet for the meaning of this foul air's designation, and the Bytes did proclaim unto me: "Helene" is an echo of the phrase "shining light," and an iteration of Helen (she with the ship launching visage). All righty then.

As for the first tidbit, referring to Helene as a "shining light" seems tone-deaf to the terrible, banshee gale it loosed upon Appalachia. Unhelpful to our search. But if we recast Helene as "the thing shining the light," we can mold its wreckage into a searchlight; pierce the existential void the storm ripped open; use the beam to find and clear the storm's psychic debris; expose the long forgotten, foundational pillars that gird our understanding of the world (the very understanding the storm has muddied). Those grand stanchions that provide the stability and order which time turns to comfort and peace; silent protectors, they keep the dizzying Kierkegaardian fear at bay. They are the *Sciences Biologic* that teach us which rhythms to dance to; the *Rules Economic* that ensure bounty is always just a screen's touch away; the *Speculative Ideologies* that offer calming comfort for consumption (available in single-serve or family-sized). So immanent, these systems invisibly guide, if not dictate, our relationship with the world.

And our searchlight reveals how far off their pedestals H.H. pushed these pillars; how close to collapse our shared-lived-experience was. There's no doubt that, Pre-Storm, I roamed jolly through clearings that my neighbors cut from the forest of all-that-is-possible; little dells where they imposed structure on their slice of life such that I could share in it. In these spaces we were magic; launching our desires into the future and following their arc eyes-closed to consummation; mindless frolics where our predictions predictably came true. If I wanted pizza I knew 828 would be there and I could call and they would answer and I'd drive there because the roads were passable and once home I could take a shower because turning-faucet = warmwater.

But Post-Storm, waking-life was a slog through formless space devoid of this stability; the pillars teetering on the edge of collapse. The absence of structure made very present the degree to which I relied upon the intentionality of others. Apparently, satisfying our ego is a communal affair. And this all became clear only because the storm sloshed everything up; cut everyone loose from their moorings; forced the body politic to stare simultaneously into the void. Wide-eyed; lit amygdala; swaying at the void's edge; anxiety's rip-current clawed at me. Will my neighbor catch me if I fall? Would I them? Will some devil hex us into believing this is the last bottle of water? Do we fight over it? Sure, maybe we share it, but right Then-There doubt reigned.

The pillars wobbled, even cracked, but the collective proved righteous; we remained upright. Fine. There's your wellspring of hope amidst the floodwaters. But this doesn't help with the fact that the storm still lurks. Like how I'm now stressing about the shade maples in the front yard. They made it through H.H., but what about the next storm? By then they'll be tall enough to breach roof, pierce torso, puncture lung. They're not trees running thick with a sap to be harvested and enjoyed. Nay! They're arboreal imps coursing dark with a spectral death.

This conflict—Past (trees = shady-calm) Vs. Present (trees = big-death-sticks)—is the Post-Storm World's defining feature. Even though those pillars haven't given way, they're straining to remain standing amidst this instability. And they'll continue to do so until the tension between Pre and Post storm is resolved. Since it was the godhead-internet's first proclamation that brought this precarious state of affairs to light, perhaps its second will reveal a solution.

You remember, the thing about Helen's eponym: that long fetishized Greek lady, Helen, with bones of purported perfection— mandible like a jib whose cut we love these centuries later; nasal bones us plebs would have to buy; bilateral zygomatic and maxilla as crisp as the sails of a Greek galley. A face of such divinity a bunch of dudes used it as an excuse to spend a decade killing. Indeed, the Trojan War's devastation was so majestic it ushered in occidental history as a thing. Its savagery so horrendous it just had to be cataloged, passed down, shared. But how actually do We remember this myth? As an object lesson about the dangers of war? A springboard to the way cooler adventures of Odysseus (cyclops, sirens, and scylla, oh my)? I fear that time has trivialized the legend; degraded its import to: "Those Greeks! What a tricky bunch with their horsey."

For true: How easy it is for a familiar narrative to conceal tragedy for so long that time lacquers it to an innocuous shine. Why worry? The Asheville Flood of 1916. The Citizen-Times ran numerous photo-essays about it in the months prior to H.H. I gaped at the sepia destruction, but only saw a static aftermath. The pictures did not sound a warning, they whispered of nature's sublime majesty. My gaze was ponderous when it needed to be penetrating. Time and forgetting muffled the lizard-brain's response, and so the 1916 storm was allowed to return in the guise of Helene. So thank you, Ms. Troy, 1190 BCE, for recalling to us the importance of locating the past within the future! If we fail to continually carry H.H. into the Post-Storm-Present—fail to maintain a clearing wherein we plant and tend the "shady-tree" of the past and the "death-tree" of the present—the storm will return with a violence equal to its forbearers. We'll never escape it; never turn this tension to peace; never synthesize that new future we seek.

Perhaps digging through H.H.'s rubble is paying off. Instead of the stereotypical "I'm gonna shove heart wrenching episodes of dread down your throat," Helene's abyss has offered up a totem or two of insight. The void is seeming like a hot stove I've just touched. I remain displeased that this monster and I must share a roof, but I also know that pies occasionally emerge from its scorching maw. I love pie. Do I love the void? [Shrug Emoji] Certainly, the storm's lessons have pushed my little raft of questioning closer to the Isle of Comfort-With-the-Abyss. But I doubt I'll reach the shore unless I turn H.H.'s searchlight onto my storm experience.

Okey-doke. My people were physically untouched. We evacuated to S.C. First time I didn't drive straight through to the beach, where land and water engage in a coked-up version of erosion that, in the mountains, unfolds at a K-hole-slow, geologic pace (is this tortoise tempo why we forgot 1916). We drove past Carowinds, its metal-toothpick rollercoasters hauling exhilarated folks to the void's edge, letting them peer over, and whisking them back to safety; the certainty of their return what they'd paid for and what Helene keeps from us. Our hotel stood next to a five-lane rife with three-story multifamily-housing, fully stocked big-boxes, corporate logos calming in their backlit familiarity, and football on the television (with Helene disaster-porn squeezed in between downs).

Life off here was as carefree as a sitcom. All those clearings we cut—where our illusion of control shines brightest—were open for business. Here, there was no doubt your plans would come true. Drive to a pub; catch the game; eat among the equally content; send thoughts and prayers to the devastated; and go home to light switches that don't sound like a clicking tongue when you flip them: "Tsk-tsk. No electric, remember?"

The normalcy smashed through me like those ancient waters had crashed through AVL. Cleaved me in two; left behind a Pre-Storm and Post-Storm Me. Used to be, if I went out for a bite and stumbled upon footage of flood or fire, I'd gawk but keep chewing; poor them, tragic that; leave a big tip for sadness' sake. But H.H. infused this simulacrum-of-tragedy with a Newtonian reality; a constant and debilitating force pressing in on all sides; felt like I was trapped deep underwater. This physical horror pinned me in a hole; held my head underwater. I couldn't see, let alone touch, my past. Rootless. I struggled to remain upright within the current of everydayness. Turn my head one way, someone's asking if they can get the dressing on the side (Is that me?). Turn the other, thirty feet of water's erasing the world wherein I kiss my wife. Bowed under the dread Helene brought; cowed by the devastation it wrought; the feckless everyday became nonsensical. The predictable and familiar became an impenetrable morass.

I'm still trudging through this Pre-Post dialectic; the storm's grip is still tight and harrowing; the pillars shaky; synthesis elusive. Like, even though potable water flows, I still get sick driving through familiar places that, having been demolished by liquid, are concurrently alien. Take The Grail (yes, it's a Monty Python thing), late of RAD. Though my memories of that space—family waiting giddy for a movie—are still so strong that the building's carcass is indiscernible, its vague shape still makes me gag a little. But: "I'm not dead yet."

Nevertheless, confronting this discomfort-with-normalcy – swallowing the nausea of memory – forced me to stop looking at the void and start looking in. It's there the treasure lay—this nascent existential understanding. And even though it's as soothing as a bed of river rock, I've seen that the pillars underneath our world-understanding stand firm; learned how our inherent goodness kept them upright amidst the storm's onslaught; and discovered how to alchemize the memory of Helene into a mortar that will gird them against future damage.

With these understandings, that kernel of NewTruth is watered; the medium of all this destruction converted into an agent of growth. May its bud flower into a subtle understanding of the earth from which it grows. May its fragrance impart a river pilot's knowledge of the tributaries that feed, and currents that move, the waters upon which we are all adrift. I'll cut you a bouquet.

Obviously, I'm still awash with worry about and hatred for the abyss (sorry about the title). But the void does seem a little less dismal (though totally and forever scary and wretched and ugly and I never want to look in it again). Since it's no longer a stranger, should I ask it over for pie? Maybe next century. Can you help me remember?

Unification
Barbara Fisher

"Unification" is part of a new series of ten, most of which were destroyed in the flood. These paintings were made up of complex layers of contradictory yet harmonious energy bursts. The chaos encountered along the way in the painting process eventually leads to integration and resolution.

My studio had 4-5 feet of water in it - there was a clear water line. Everything was upside down and piled up in the mud. This painting was hanging on the wall just above the waterline. It was mud splattered, but not too hard to clean up. I was able to save a few this way. All the work that was underwater was ruined. This painting about chaos and integration survived the chaos that was Helene.

Helene: This Lady Was No Saint!
Jeanne Charters

Such a lovely name. A saint's name, actually, and the name of my first mother-in-law. She was Helene Charters, a woman I knew to be a walking saint herself.

The news warned of a big wind that week. What's to be afraid of, I mused? Here I am in Asheville, North Carolina, far removed from the coast—a town celebrated as a climate haven in this time of environmental change and challenge. I had worried about my daughter in California, land of quaking earth and raging wildfires. But Asheville? With its sky-high mountains and glorious forests? Not a chance. Everyone says so. It must be safe here.

On September 26, the night before Helene visited, I hosted a going-away party for an elderly and much-loved neighbor who was moving away to be near family. I went to bed after the party and removed my state-of-the-art, five-thousand-dollar hearing aids—the first that have ever worked on my genetically defective ears which had ceased to do their job (i.e., hear) when I was forty. And that was many, many years ago (don't ask). Suffice it to say, I've spent half my life saying, "huh?"

After downing a relaxing elixir, I closed my eyes and slept. The next day, I learned the wind was howling like a banshee around my little house that night. And I mean wind! Which, of course, I could not hear. I read much later—when I had access to news—that the storm reached more than forty mph gusts. I heard nothing, and Archie, my alarm clock Yorkie, was kenneled that night because of the party. I can always depend on him to warn me in a frenzy of barking at any noise or disturbance, determined to use all of his eleven pounds to protect my life and limb against danger. But he wasn't there that night. Only old, deaf me!

I woke up early the next morning and noticed there was no clock lighted on my nightstand. Hmmm, power outage. I picked up my cell to check the news and learned very quickly that cell service was also down. I couldn't call my husband at the Veterans Home in Black Mountain who lives there now due to Alzheimer's. I was frightened as word spread that the area had been devastated.

When I turned on the spigot the water came out—brown. Hmmm, maybe there's a bottle of water in the car. There was, and it tasted divine.

However, when I opened the garage door, there were huge, downed trees covering my driveway and the street. OMG, this is bad. But, not to worry, the city will clear those out of our way by nightfall. Only days later, when traveling the streets of my town, did I realize how many driveways and streets were buried in fallen timber. And how impossible was the task of clearing them quickly.

But there are angels. The grandson of an elderly man up the hill who, realizing his grandfather was out of life-saving oxygen, marshaled an army of friends from Candler to come over to our neighborhood with chainsaws to clear us out so they could take him to the hospital. How do you thank people for that? I tried, but there are not words powerful enough to express how deeply grateful I felt to them.

I am lucky that my range is gas so I could light it with a lighter and cook myself a burger from my freezer. Ah yes, but there was another rub—a freezer and refrigerator full of food—that would only last a day or two before it would have to be tossed out.

The word spread quickly through the neighborhood. Publix had ice! Now that the driveway was cleared, I got out and headed there. There was a limit to how many bags I could get, but scoring ice felt like winning the lottery. An old ice chest in the garage saved some of the food and kept me fed for another day.

Night came early. It was September after all, so by seven that evening it was pitch black.

Helene: This Lady Was No Saint!

The next day, standing outside of Publix for cell service, I was able to contact my daughters to tell them that I was alive. The Veterans Home was still unreachable, but there was a text from their corporate owners that the patients were safe. Whew, an angel corporation!

Night came again very early and, again, I lay in the dark wondering about everything.

Time to toss the food. Stuff was melted. I pulled two pounds of bacon from the freezer, cooked it, and took it to the streets. Neighbors I never saw before smelled it and surrounded me in minutes for a piece. I felt like Lady Bountiful and the bacon was gone in three minutes flat. Again, no way to reach the Veterans Home and water was scarce.

After another dark and scary night alone, I made a decision. Screw this. I cannot face another twenty-four hours of this aloneness and quiet. Fortunately, I had gassed my car before the storm, so that was good. I made it to the kennel and got Archie out; and, though the major routes to High Rock Lake were not in operation, with the help of my angel GPS. The normally three-hour trip took six hours due to road destruction. To family, to light—to water—to television where the images of what I had escaped haunted my every waking hour.

I was so lucky. Many people in my county perished during Helene. Washed away into the rivers or buried in the mud of landslides. One family in Fairview, where I used to live, lost eleven members.

Only weeks later did we begin to realize the toll of Helene. There are still people missing—perhaps buried in mud or washed away never to be found. My heart hurts for the artists with masterpieces destroyed, for the restaurant workers without income for weeks, for FEMA personnel who worked in mud and raging water to save the endangered while being maligned for political purposes, and for my beautiful Asheville which I know will be restored. Someday.

Helene was no lady—and certainly, no saint. She was a raging harridan bent on destruction and death. Hopefully, she was a once-in-a-century tourist who will never return in my lifetime, or yours.

Bouquet #3
Kevin Andrew

Attempting to detach and focus on creating a bouquet of flowers. I failed. I cannot suppress or bury my feelings for our community, for our country. There is hope throughout this painting, but I know better than to try to disengage. Explosions of emotion, gentle reminders of hope, and a flood of layers all showed themselves within this work.

lit by stars
a poem for when the power returns
Jenna Lindbo

if you walk outside in the velvety black of morning
look up
shield your eyes from the newly revived streetlamps
and possibly– when you soften your gaze, you will find
tree limbs lit by stars
twinkling in their outstretched arms
resting in upturned palms
glowing like candles behind cupped hands, standing vigil
shimmering along branches bespoke with invisible threads
constellations blurred, blotted out, obscured by silhouettes
leaves and limbs, some already bare
twining overhead with the unheard music of morning
like dancers at a silent disco, still more reaching out
steady, humble, broken, wise
hopeful, reluctant, eager, calloused and tender
hands raised without a word, saying
here
i am here
we're still here

attendance well before dawn
following helene, this unspoken roll call with the stars
        and the trees feels sacred
but isn't it always?
life and death awaiting our attention
a new day, this next breath
a standing invitation to presence
to *tend, attend, and dance* with aliveness
senses awakened, in attendance
present

as we welcome back electricity
and with gratitude as temperatures fall below freezing
let us pause before flipping a switch to remember the absence
of light, the presence of love, and fear, and courage
pause to remember those who labored, unseen
to light our homes and power appliances
from the electric kettle to the kitchen radio, the one we scrambled
        to find and huddled beside
from the refrigerator to the wifi router, phone chargers
        to dehumidifiers
now buzzing, working overtime

pause to remember those still waiting for power to be restored
waiting for potable water to flow through repaired pipes
pause to remember those who have been displaced

lit by stars, a poem for when the power returns

who have lost their lives, loved ones, livelihoods
the road home washed out, dreams knocked from foundations,
        and the many
still waiting for a place to call home, for help rebuilding
for shelter from the cold, a sanctuary
of loving community, a place of belonging, people to share with
resources, warm meals, stories, grief, laughter, song
decadent joy and giant sorrow

pause and remember gathering
the sudden and spontaneous drawing near to one another
becoming closer, the pulse of human connection
        growing steadily, stronger
together with great softness
lantern hearts beckoning, *here!*
come, this way, we are here
beacons in the long night of unknown

instead of being driven by electric lights and
        the persistent pace of doing
caught in the wheels of capitalism, consumption, isolation,
        and instant gratification
let us remember a different rhythm, an ancient groove guided
        by nature
the sun, the moon, a deeper
knowing in our bones

remember the soft light, lantern hearts aglow
remember to lean in, listen, and slow down
help us remember neighbors helping neighbors,
         the felt sense of reciprocity,
mutual aid, generous offerings, the abundance of care
when the world returns, should we ever return
remember that "normal" is a myth

moving forward
help us remember radical times and radical people
being human
remember to rest, reach
out, ask for what we need, share what we have to give,
         lift each other up
let our eyes adjust– and truly see one another
friends, neighbors, loved ones, the stranger, reshaped
rivers and lakes, these mountains, the extraordinary planet
         we call home, and tree limbs
lit by stars

Summer Bouquet
Linda Girardi

I had just hung this mosaic art in my gallery at Foundation Studios. It took nearly 80 hours to make and was the best piece I'd ever done! Foundation was located about 100 yards from the French Broad River, so when the river rose during Helene, the floodwaters submerged the studio. After the water receded, I went into the collapsing building several times to look for this piece but couldn't locate it in the piles of mud and debris. Working with other artists in the studio, we did manage to salvage hundreds of other artworks, inspiring this poem (next section).

Before the Resurrection
also by Linda Girardi

Today the city crews are cleaning trees. It takes a special
tool to pluck the plastic garlands and looping wires.
Easy to untangle the fabric, harder the metal sheaths.
How will they clean the leaves
encrusted with river silt,
leaves that have turned from green to grey,
leaves that have fallen outside the shattered studios
where we stand knee-deep in mud, handing
warped canvases from one person to another.

Amateur archeologists, we unearth bottles of wine,
strands of clay beads, still-perfect pots.
We work so perfectly together, an assembly line of efficiency,
until we smell, through paper masks, meat frying
two buildings over. One by one we meander over,
wait patiently for a plain hamburger on a hard roll.
No meal has ever tasted better.

We stand together without words.
We have no words for this.
The line now broken, the artists leave,
stacking scarred art in car trunks
like gurneys into an ambulance.

Here the outline of a white dove, here a blindfolded girl.
So many pictures of mountains and sunsets,
so many bouldered roads that trail off into the distance,
into the unknown.

Oteen
Eva Murray

When Brian and I poked our heads out our front doors, next to each other, the last rain drops of Helene were falling. No one had slept much for two days on our neighborhood hill in Oteen, rain a barrage of pellets.

Then we marveled. As we looked around in a daze, and from our decks, we saw that not one shingle, window, car on our two properties was damaged. We expected destruction.

"Amazing," I said. The stillness in Oteen was eerie.

"It's like Katrina," Brian said. "I've never been in a hurricane before."

"Me neither. I've been through a few tornadoes," I said, Midwesterner by birth. "And one flood." I'm 65, so I have more than a few years on Brian.

Below our decks, we could see cars trying to drive on Swannanoa River Road. They were met with police cruisers, blocking the road 24/7 as flood waters had risen. The next day, the National Guard appeared by truck, and we heard their helicopters overhead. Crews cleared the road, chains grinding on my fallen trees.

We couldn't leave Oteen hill, the only way out blocked by a fallen wall. Firefighters came right away to clear a lane, and Brian let all the neighbors know. Once I could leave, I explored South Tunnel Road off Swannanoa leading to Black Mountain, where a car teetered, frozen, suspended in tree branches.

And for the week to come, Brian did what Brian always does. He made sure I had enough food for a few days. He toted buckets of water from the creek below and boiled water on his outdoor grill for washing and drinking. He brought food and pineapples from the restaurant he manages, Red Lobster. He cooked sausages and eggs on his grill, for all of us on Oteen, folks in six houses and mobile homes up the hill. And for his employees at Red Lobster. But without cell service, water or power, I decided to evacuate for a week in a hotel in Johnson City, TN. I was reimbursed immediately by FEMA.

Brian says he's just being a good neighbor. Since we moved into our houses the same weekend in March 2022, Brian has been there for me, always, only a text away. He carries heavy packages into my house and installs window shades. We text each other when wifi or the power is out. He introduced himself on our first weekend of being next-door neighbors with, "I just want to be a good neighbor to you." I thought I was in a Hallmark movie.

He's the guardian angel of Oteen. I told him he deserves an award, and he demurred. I've nominated him for the Neighborhood Volunteer Spotlight, sponsored by the City of Asheville's Neighborhood Advisory Committee. I will surprise him with it when he wins. Brian moved fast in the aftermath, as fast as the people of Asheville, rebuilding a new city out of the mud and destruction, a new way forward.

Ridgelines Rise
Erin Kellem

It took me weeks to find my creativity after Hurricane Helene, resulting first in this piece. The colors are somber in comparison to my cobalts and teals that I love to play with, but every time I
reached for those favorite colors, they were just not right. These
mountains are burdened, and though you can see only the ridgelines,
the valleys are scarred.

Discovering Life at the Bone
Porter Taylor

September 27, 2024, Hurricane Helene came to Asheville, with some areas receiving over 30 inches of rain, and the French Broad River cresting at over 30 feet. As a result, those of us who live here had to find a new way not just to live but to survive.

I thought about that because Hurricane Helene pushed all residents into the woods to simplify their lives whether they wanted to or not. My wife Jo and I lost electricity, our basement had six inches of water, and our favorite maple tree crashed in our front yard.

As a Jesus follower, I am ashamed to say for a time I found myself in the land of despair. I felt like Jesus when he cried, "My God My God Why have you forsaken me?" Yes, I know that's a ridiculous comparison, but that's what can happen when you are overwhelmed by nature and completely unable to turn the outer world around. As a result, you can forget that all you can do and are called to do, is to reorient the inner world. Until you do that, you forget how to take the first step and then the next and the next.

For me, the first step is gratitude. "This is the day the Lord has made, let us rejoice and be glad in it. (Psalm 18:24)." Did we lose a lot because of this storm? Yes. Our daughter was supposed to be married Saturday, three days after the storm began. Her friend from England came to Asheville, her fiancé's family from Ohio and Colorado and more. Then there's the many lost homes and more importantly the many lost lives in this part of the state. Maybe life is sweetest only when you realize how fragile life can be.

What's more, I have also never seen such kindness. As the poet Naomi Shahib Nye wrote in *Kindness*: "Before you know what kindness really is/you must lose things, feel the future dissolve in a moment like salt in a weakened broth." Here, it's people opening their homes for others they barely know. Men and women volunteering to distribute water and food, and just a sense of community because all of us have experienced anxiety and loss.

So, this is part of what I have learned:

▸ Take nothing for granted, especially tomorrow.

▸ Think about the relationships that have remained weakened, the friends I have let slip away. I feel called to make amends or simply to catch up.

▸ Focus on the things that have been postponed. For me, it's the book I keep saying I will finish writing as well as the books I keep avoiding reading. Plus, it's the classes I have thought about teaching but have not followed through.

▸ Erase the distance that I have allowed to take place between me and God. Increase and deepen my prayer life. Focus on the ways in which I have let relationships falter, especially my relationship with God.

However, I keep remembering the last words of St. Francis of Assisi: "Let's begin again." Because the past is the past, and this is the only day we have to be alive.

Therefore, I now think God is calling me to take steps that are deeper and wider. I am working on a new book. I am reaching out to my children. I am seeking to lessen my anxiety about my own health issues and instead give thanks for this day and the things I remember in it. I am praying more for the politicians who I believe can help this nation to work and thinking less about those whom I believe cannot. I haven't watched any television since the storm came and intend to monitor the amount post storm and instead read more. I am seeking to increase my gratitude for everything instead of dwelling in criticism. I hope to embrace a no-labels way of seeing people—regardless of their politics, religion, social standing, education, race, gender, and on and on.

As Henry Daivd Thoreau wrote about 175 years ago in his book *Walden*: "It is life near the bone where it is sweetest." He also wrote, "I went to the woods because I wished to live deliberately, to front only the essential facts of life…. I did not wish to live what was not life, living is so dear …. Simplicity, simplicity, simplicity! I say let your affairs be two or three, and not a hundred or a thousand."

These words keep running in my brain. If I have learned anything from Hurricane Helene, it's that indeed I too do "not wish to live what was not life." Therefore, this day that I am alive is the only day I have to be connected to the living God who enables me to be connected to my true self and my fellow human beings. May my memory of Hurricane Helene help me remember this.

Last Dance

Cheryl Keefer

A week before the storm, I found myself in Old Fort, North Carolina under a glorious blue sky. The day felt timeless, serene. Drawn to Irma's Produce market, I hoped to find the last peaches of the season—and I did. They were perfectly sweet, a fleeting taste of summer.

What truly captured me, though, were the dahlias. Towering white and pink blossoms framed the entrance to the market, gleaming in the sunlight like a celebration of life itself. I couldn't resist their beauty. I lingered, took photos, sketched them in my mind, and then spent all of the next Thursday painting them as rain poured relentlessly outside. There was something ironic about it, almost foreboding.

By Friday, the rains had done their work. The dahlias were gone, drowned along with the field they'd brightened and the market they'd adorned. What I had painted just days before—a vivid celebration of life—was now a memory of something lost.

Thirst
Rebecca Beck

The night of the storm, solid sheets of rain fell and fell, low-toned as a duet of bassoons and cellos. Wind pounded the windows in rapid, percussive beats. Peering outside, I couldn't tell if it was the golden hue of the porch light or the moon revealing the exotic dancing of the white oaks, maples, and hickories. The melodic rain, the swaying trees, the aggressive wind seemed to promise a spectacular, glistening morning. I smiled at the thought of opening the door to the smell of damp leaves and sweet ozone.

My awe shifted to worry as the wind gained more power and rain pummeled the windows in violent bullets. The trees, no longer swaying, clacked together in angry bursts followed by eerie bouts of stillness. How long could they endure their torment? I pictured one, maybe more, landing on the house. I wondered where my husband and I would be safest—the basement? Maybe the small bathroom off the kitchen? Should we put on bike helmets? I tried to picture what to do to protect our golden retriever. As my worries soared, in my head, I designed a helmet for dogs (you can laugh at the image) then chastised myself for not staying focused on viable survival strategies. Were we safer in the basement? There could be flooding. We should be upstairs, away from rising water. But if a tree fell on the roof, we'd be vulnerable there.

Three, maybe four hours passed. Wide awake, as the rain continued, I obsessed over deforestation, too much construction on steep slopes, the intensification of storms as the earth warms. Did we have adequate tree coverage to hold the earth above our home in place? Denial set in, a vehicle for hardening myself against panic. I actually fell asleep for a while. When there's nowhere to go, when nature is out of control, surrender may be the only response.

The following morning, I stepped onto our porch into a silence that was too quiet—no distant cars or trucks, no neighbor's air compressor or tractor. I walked into the yard to check on my newly planted toad lilies. Their delicate buds had faced down the storm and won. If flowers could prevail, I assumed our community was unscathed, too. In that moment, I didn't realize we were situated in a miraculous oasis.

I returned to the kitchen, and my husband came in to tell me that at least four of our treasured, old white oaks had fallen. Like carrots being pulled effortlessly from soft garden loam, their roots simply gave way in Helene's fists. We would realize later that the presence of massive, exposed networks of roots on our property foreshadowed our region's terrible story.

We decided to walk up the road. Another towering tree had fallen on our neighbors' carport and from what we could see, at least one of their vehicles was crushed. Further along, power lines dangled like holiday garlands over the street. In the sunlight, they almost looked festive. A couple we didn't recognize strolled from the woods looking dazed. Turned out they were staying in the neighboring Airbnb. "Are storms normally like this here?" they asked. I couldn't quite understand what they meant by *like this.*

Further down the road, we ran into our neighbors. They had found their retro transistor radio, and in her typically gentle way, Sarah broke the news that entire neighborhoods had been wiped out . . . entire towns washed away in the terrible synergy of torrential rains, heavy winds, landslides, unleashed floods. Swannanoa, where we live, was among the hardest hit. I reached down to pet our dog, Hattie, but ended up wrapping my arms around her, holding my hammering heart against her broad, silken flank. Walls of water pouring down the ring of lush, timeless mountains that circle the green bowl of our valley was beyond anything I could imagine. I reached up for my husband's hand. I finally understood that what we experienced was unprecedented. People across the country were seeing images of the devastation. Without power or internet, we couldn't see what they were seeing, and in retrospect, I'm grateful that for a while, I was ignorant of that.

Two days after the storm, we left the area for a few days to regroup. While tucked safely in a rented bungalow, we finally saw the images we'd been unable to imagine while in their midst, and our hearts broke anew with each viewing.

Now that we're back home after two weeks away, we're still without power and water. We regularly visit the relief station in our local grocery store parking lot. I want to hug the huge, glimmering, stainless steel cylinder that is the potable water truck. We are overwhelmed with a sense of gratitude for it and for the open-hearted people who help us there.

In my kitchen, I heat some of the fresh "truck" water in our overused electric tea kettle, then sit with my back to the laundry tub as my husband pours it over my hair. He guides my hand to the shampoo bottle that sits out of my sightline. These days, my hair is longer than it has ever been and it trails into the sink. He holds it up when he rinses it.

Using water this way, to wash dishes, cook, and bathe, brings me closer to my great-grandmothers—farm women—who routinely fed their chrome and enamel stoves the dried oak and hickory needed to heat water they poured into galvanized tubs for bathing their children—my grandparents. Washing clothes in those tubs, running them through a ringer, their fingertips stiff and bone white as they hung them to dry . . . I think of all those hours spent with those mundane tasks as I bathe at the sink, knowing my routine is temporary.

Three weeks passed. Our water quality was raised to "boil before cooking or drinking." Still, I obsess over water quality and can't bring myself to use it, even if first boiled, for washing vegetables, filling a pasta pot, showering. Beneath the earth's surface, guided by its contours and changes in elevation, at times diverted by impermeable layers of rock, groundwater charts its own convoluted course along a path of least resistance. After the flooding and landslides shuffled the earth, in what ways was our groundwater forced to forge new pathways? What new substances did it pick up along its untested route? How much of it ended up in our reservoirs? I'm plagued with these questions. I address the unknown in small ways, don't let my dog—who walked through washed-up-dirt from the creek—into the house without first luring her into a kiddie pool filled with mild soap and potable water. She loves it, doesn't realize I'm trying to preserve her good health.

We still stock up on potable water from the water truck at the relief center. Even though we have plenty of it, I'm so thirsty. Am I projecting my anxiety onto the physical sensation of thirst? If so, what am I thirsting for? I'm guessing trust. Trust that before too long, I'll be able to turn on the tap and feel assured that the water is safe. In the shower, I'll let it pour over my head without worrying that untested toxins might seep through my pores.

On election day, we continued to be without clean tap water. I met a woman and her four young children in line to vote. The youngest, maybe in kindergarten, clung to her side. I asked the mom the ubiquitous question everyone seemed to be asking of people they didn't know—"How are you doing?" She told me she'd been sound asleep when the floodwater rushed through their front door. Her oldest, a light sleeper, woke her up. It became clear to her that she and her children would have to swim to safety. As they waded in chest-high water through their living room, the youngest lost his footing. Seeing it happen, her oldest didn't hesitate to dive into the turbid water to raise his sibling up. The reality that a woman and her four little ones swam out of their house through a torrent of rain and wind to safety, has not stopped reverberating in my head. They made a miracle. Each time I recall our conversation, I feel the same incredulous awe over their dauntless grit.

The woman recounted the event with such cheer, such awe and gratitude, that I wondered if maybe she was still in shock. But reflecting and healing require time, an unassailable luxury these days when the simple tasks of hauling water, obtaining food, getting her kids to school bathed, fed, and ready to learn, surely consume all of it. Now, instead of a comfortable, warm home, they live in a camper in her friend's backyard. Her story is a miracle to celebrate; I pray it doesn't become a timeless haunting.

This woman's story embodies for me the devastation that our region continues to experience and yet is so difficult to fathom. I drive down Tunnel Road in Swannanoa and see homes folded in on themselves, a huge tankard wedged up against a tree on the river's edge. Piles of lumber, trees, smashed furniture line the road. Still, I can't fully extrapolate the ruin I witness in front of me to the entirety of human loss and suffering occurring across our region. Yet after my conversation with her, I have a clearer lens for projecting her terror and suffering onto others who were forced to swim through raging water, the reality of children saving each other, and the terror of victims who had to wait for rescue in the absence of a way to communicate.

The need for emotional healing in our community is as massive as the physical ruin Helene left behind. We witness so much generosity—warmly and lovingly shared. May that support expand across multiple types of needs—emotional, spiritual, and physical—and endure long after the water trucks depart.

Villanelle for Helene
Sondra Hall

Ill used, I will destroy
In perfect time and measure
   Ralph Waldo Emerson

You cannot fold a flood and put it in your drawer
   Emily Dickinson

Dears, there is no lucky star,
Wishing won't change a thing.
I am the river; I leave a scar.

Believe me when I tell you, hard
—I flatten all that stands,
Dears, there is no lucky star.

Tell it on the mountain, go!
Her trees all bent and buckled
I am the river; I leave a scar.

Wish upon the darkest night
Jet black and absent light
Dears, there is no lucky star.

Ill used, I will destroy
In perfect time and measure
I am the river; I leave a scar.

Boulders like marbles roll
Bodies, branches tangle
Dears, there is no lucky star,
I am the river; I leave a scar.

Acknowledgements

I gratefully acknowledge the writers and artists who contributed their work to this collection and patiently responded to my editing comments. Special thanks to artist Erin Kellem, who introduced me to her fellow River Arts District artists. Elizabeth Schulte Ross, Peggy Sauter, and Dr. Beth Goode edited the sections I wrote, and Debbie Scholl proofread the entire book. Any errors are mine.

Gretchen Horn, co-owner of Malaprop's Bookstore/Cafe in downtown Asheville, North Carolina, graciously shared key aspects of book marketing. Book expert Lauren Harr, co-founder of Gold Leaf Literary in Asheville, introduced me to Gretchen and provided helpful advice.

Brandon Zamudio and Wayne Erbsen patiently answered questions about administrative details needed to produce this book.

Others were not directly involved in the book yet provided much-needed help. My fellow Presidential Leadership Scholars sent heaters, tents, warm clothing, camp stoves, and more for me to distribute to the community, and provided love and encouragement. A special shout-out to An-Me Chung, Traci Scott, Katie McNerney, Micaela McMurrough, Dr. Sheril Kirshenbaum, Irela Bagué, Neha Misra, Will McNulty, Ben Teague, Holly Gordon, Ginny Buckingham, AnnMaura Connolly, Cassie Farrelly, Kevin Adler, Dr. Neil Grunberg, as well as those who donated funds anonymously to groups helping with the recovery.

When delivery trucks couldn't make it to my house to bring the donated supplies, dear friend Pam Klotz and her husband Mark graciously accepted packages at their house and Pam's kind-hearted daughter Kim Smith (not the same person as the artist whose work is in this book with a similar name) brought them to my doorstep.

Other out-of-town friends provided encouragement and help, especially Connecticut friends Val Messineo and her husband Eric

Bengtson. Like many heroes from across the country, Eric drove to our area with power tools and a smile, joining several of the countless work crews here to help across the region. I am grateful to all who have helped, and are helping, with the recovery effort.

I thank my neighbors, who continue to work together beautifully to persevere.

Thanks to the kind-hearted staff at Lake Todd Fish Camp in Concord, North Carolina who treated me like family. Three weeks after the storm, I had driven a couple hours east in search of a place to do laundry and marvel over indoor showers and toilets that flushed without needing to fill the tank manually. I arrived at their restaurant as an exhausted stranger. I left with a full stomach and a full heart, better prepared to return home the next morning.

Thank you to Dr. Jennifer Werely. Without her expert guidance and kindness during an earlier unrelated medical crisis, I wouldn't have been able to complete this book or, well, do much of anything.

Most of all, I thank my dear family: My children Ashley, Kevin, and Bradley, their kids and partners, and my extended family. I also proudly count as family of course the Sarr/Njie family and, in West Africa, the Starfish International family. Family members helped sort out options for dealing with the aftermath and kept my spirits up. As always, they bring me joy and enrich my life in more ways than I can count.

My apologies to anyone I have inadvertently failed to mention. Pulling together a book—and recovering after a disaster—is a group effort, and I am grateful to all who helped.

Shelley McKechnie
Asheville, North Carolina
January 2025

Contributors

Kevin Andrew
As a Lifelong Creative, Andrew followed the *right path* for many years before questioning it. After obtaining undergraduate and graduate degrees in Civil Engineering, years working in IT Corporate America, and a successful Entrepreneur Business Exit, Andrew now paints abstract artwork full time with intention and a business mindset. Creating art is a journey to find his *self*. Andrew's artwork is an abstraction of sensations and emotions which connects with collectors on a visceral, relatable level. Being vulnerable and open about his work helps him better understand his purpose. creativekevin.com

Rebecca Beck
Rebecca Beck lives in Swannanoa, North Carolina. She typically writes fiction, but after experiencing Hurricane Helene, she was moved to portray the region's suffering to those living outside the area. Rebecca's work was long-listed for the 2022 Thomas Wolfe Fiction Prize (short fiction) and the 2022 Tucson Festival of Books Literary Awards. Her short stories appear in the January 2024 issue of *Action, Spectacle, The Great Smokies Review, 34th Parallel Magazine, Glint Literary Journal,* and *Grub Street Literary Magazine.* Her poetry appears in various small presses. Rebecca is also at work on a second novel while seeking an agent for her first.

Jaime Byrd
Jaime Byrd is a US-based contemporary artist with an Emmy nomination in film editing. She's known for her landscape paintings which capture the emotional energy of nature from around the globe and has created an innovative blend of filmmaking and technology that brings her artwork to life with video and technology. jaimebyrd.com

Jeanne Charters
Jeanne Charters moved from New York State to Asheville after a long and successful career in television. She became a regular contributor to *WNC Woman* magazine with her column, "Funny, isn't it?" until the magazine ceased publication. Then, she decided to become a novelist. To date, she has published four novels: *Yellow* (a scathing story about the TV industry), *Shanty Gold,* a re-imagining of her great grandmother's immigration from Ireland during the 19th century Great Famine; followed by *Lace Curtain* and *Silk Stocking.* She is currently writing her fifth novel--a multi-generational tale of challenges faced by strong women in today's America. jeannecharters.com

Lee Davies
Lee Davies is a graphic designer and visual artist residing in Asheville, NC. As member of the LGBTQ+ community, he strives for inclusivity and intersectionality in artistic voices throughout the Blue Ridge. During the hurricane aftermath, he helped host eclectic potlucks, bringing together a neighborhood's quickly thawing fridge contents, finally putting the plasticware hoarded from takeout orders to good use.

Terry Leigh Deal
Terry is a naturalist and environmental educator who has taught in both private and public schools in the Asheville area for over thirty years. She is a mother of three and a grandmother to two children, all of whom are Asheville natives. Terry has a Bachelor of Arts and Teaching Certification from the University of Florida and a Master of Science in Educational Studies and Environmental Education from the University of Utah. Her writing passions include creative non-fiction and poetry.

Contributors

Debbie DeWall

Debbie DeWall is a California transplant who writes and plays golf. She lives in Laurel Park, North Carolina with her husband and three cats. This is her first hurricane.

Gail S. Drozd

A native of Michigan, Gail has always been a maker. As a young girl learning to sew, she discovered how cutting fabric apart and sewing it back together in a new way made for endless possibilities. That same approach, using a vast array of materials, has been her life's work. In her career as a graphic designer, assembling images with words was the mainstay of her creative life. She also loved the art of stained glass–again cutting apart and piecing together. Other beloved materials have included: hardwood for furniture making, steel for welding functional art, and currently oil and acrylic paint. Represented by ashevillegalleryofart.com. gaildrozd.com

Wayne Erbsen

Wayne Erbsen is currently a professor of Appalachian Music at the University of North Carolina at Asheville. He has worked as a book publisher, author, musician, NPR radio host and recording artist. His newest book is *Southern Mountain Music, The Collected Writings of Wayne Erbsen.* He makes his home in Asheville, North Carolina.

Barbara Fisher

Fisher was born in New York City, educated in Colorado and California, and lived for many years on the West coast before settling in Asheville, North Carolina in 1998. Her work has been exhibited throughout the country and is in many collections, including the Asheville Art Museum. She describes her work in general as "transforming interior narratives into a visual language."

Linda Girardi

Linda Girardi is a writer, artist, and teacher specializing in fused and mosaic glass, fiber art, and jewelry. After a 37-year career in environmental policy and communications, she retired to Asheville where she translates her interests in natural and urban environments into art and poetry. elementalartstudio.com.

Chrys Corn Goodman

Chrys Corn Goodman is an intuitive figurative-abstract painter who works primarily in oil and mixed media. Her art is created by responding to the mixing of differing art mediums, listening to songwriters, and contemplating history or memories and emotional or spiritual truths. She lives and works in the Blue Ridge Mountains near Asheville, North Carolina. chryscorn.com, Instagram: @chryscorn

Sondra Hall

Sondra Hall is a long-time educator who founded "Take My Word For It!" to provide creative writing adventures for elementary and middle school kids. TMWFI sparked the imaginations of hundreds of students in the San Francisco Bay area, Boston, and northern Virginia. She currently teaches adult creative writing classes through her program, Escape to the Page, privately, in local community colleges, and through the Osher Lifelong Learning Institute. Sondra holds a BA in Art History from Tufts University and an MA in Creative Arts Therapy from Lesley University. She's delighted by antique objects that hold stories, leafy plants, poems, and iced coffee with cream.

Ann Harris

A long-time steward of the land, Ann Harris resides in a forest next to the Blue Ridge Parkway, where she nurtures a deep connection to nature. Her co-residents are two teen sons, two trail-loving dogs, and a family of black bears. Her background includes directing wilderness-based programs with North Carolina Outward Bound and earning an M.A. in Education Leadership, where she explored imaginative methods to enhance learning. Ann has founded and led schools, worked within international schools and local public institutions, and conducted policy analysis to improve educational systems. Currently, she keeps busy by restoring the forest that was damaged by the hurricane, as well as helping folks find the motivation to keep striving. jabberwockypedagogy.com

MB Holloway
M.B. grew up in West Virginia; rode wanderlust to the right-angle north-east; retreated to a late-shift prodigal son bit in western North Carolina; was saved by a woman of boundless affection, bottomless concern, damning sensitivity, matchless beauty, and unequalled humor; also she humble. Instagram: @avl_esq

Cheryl Keefer
John Keats wrote, "Beauty is truth, truth beauty," and Keefer embraces this philosophy in her art. As a modern impressionist, she paints a wide variety of subjects, from sunlit bouquets and outdoor cafés to sweeping landscapes. Working primarily in oils, Keefer often paints en plein air, capturing the play of light and atmosphere. Urban scenes intrigue her, with glowing lights and rain-soaked streets, while nature inspires her with its quiet majesty. Through her paintings, Keefer aims to spark memories, evoke emotion, and invite viewers to experience the beauty of life with fresh eyes and renewed wonder.

Erin Kellem
Erin Kellem is a mixed media artist living in Asheville, North Carolina. After 30+ years as a fine art photographer, she has turned to mixed media. Erin's artistic fascination with light is carried over from her previous work in photography. She experiments with the play of highlights and shadows in landscapes, clouds, and water, and how those elements influence color. Her newest series explores the

luminosity of clouds. Made of pigment-enhanced resin, each piece employs multiple layers of varying transparency to explore the way shifting light reveals the nuances of cloud formations.

Kate Krause
Kate Krause is a singer-songwriter, author of two books, worship leader, teacher, and life coach. She traveled the world for fourteen years sharing her music and stories. She has played and taught everywhere from castles in Germany to remote villages in India. She lives with her family in a cabin that her husband built in Fairview, North Carolina. She has her own business teaching music lessons to all ages, including sponsorship students from low-income families. You can find out more about her and her music at katehurley.com and read her writing at prodigalmind.org

Jenny Lee
Jenny Lee is a military brat born in Spain, and raised in Georgia, Illinois, Maryland and also Hendersonville, North Carolina, where she currently lives with her dog, Sunny. A huge theater buff, she's lived and "done theater" in Atlanta and Seattle. She's currently writing flash fiction about mermaids. This is her first hurricane.

Jenna Lindbo
Singer. Songwriter. Dog-lover. Jenna Lindbo is a lyrical poet, performer, and multi-instrumentalist with a gift for deepening connection and inspiring creative expression in groups. She lives in East Asheville and her effervescent spirit is contagious, whether on or off stage! Blending her musical talents and natural flair for facilitation, she is a skilled leader, designing programs and infusing gatherings with poetry and song to anchor learning, spark imagination, and encourage integration and embodiment.

Contributors

Cynthia Llanes

Cynthia Llanes discovered a love of art at an early age. After completing her BA in Fine Arts, she pursued a career as a textile designer in the Los Angeles fashion district and later became active in the Los Angeles art scene, joining art exhibitions. Llanes calls her move from California to beautiful western North Carolina an inspirational awakening because of the way it motivated her to paint outdoors. "Every day nature's phenomena reflect back to us its beauty in magical and dramatic images. My work is a celebration and an expression of my wonder of the natural world." Llane's work can be found in private collections in the United States. cynthiallanesartist.com

Brian Longacre

Identity's a hard thing to pin down and an even harder thing to pen down, but a few of the edge pieces that make up the 1000-piece puzzle that is me include teacher, husband, father, fool, and wordworker. I have known Asheville and have been inspired by her for 31 years, and I have known her to be a resplendent, fierce, creative, and independent woman to me, so what Helene did to her feels unconscionable. To saturate her, flood her, then cut her off from water for weeks is cruel. But aSHEville is strong, and her strength is ancient.

Shelley McKechnie

Shelley McKechnie lives in Asheville where she's writing a book about how long-distance biking helped her successfully recover from severe injuries sustained in a car accident. She holds a BA in English from Cornell University and an MBA from the University of Chicago and has long alternated between writing, photography, community service, and running businesses. She is currently collaborating to extend the greenway network in western North Carolina.

Eva Murray

Eva Murray's story *Freelancing in the Land of Gentry* appeared in *Tryst* in 2009; *Cualquiera* in *The Rambler*, 2005; and *Warm Hands, Grub Street*, 1995. Her stories are collected in *Something Came Over Me* (2025). The first chapter of her novel, *The Odyssey of Izzy*, was a finalist in *Barrelhouse Magazine's* "Office Life" short fiction contest in 2009. She has also published articles about such artists as B.B. King, Stephane Grappelli, Etta James, Bobby McFerrin, and Buckwheat Zydeco. In 2006, she spoke on KALW-X in the San Francisco Bay Area about her photojournalism, *Seeking San Francisco* (2013). She earned an M.F.A. in Fiction Writing from Sarah Lawrence College.

Brian Railsback

Brian Railsback, a Professor of English at Western Carolina University, served as founding Dean of The Honors College and Chair of the Faculty there. He teaches creative writing and U.S. literature. He has published a novel, short stories, scholarly books, and numerous essays. He has lectured or taught courses in Cuba, Georgia, Hungary, Japan, Mexico, Morocco, and Portugal. A Fiction Participant at the Bread Loaf Writers Conference, in 2023 he was named the Steve Kemp Writer in Residence at Great Smoky Mountains National Park; his essays about living there are in the Fall 2024 issue of *Smokies Life Journal*.

Elizabeth Schulte Roth

Elizabeth Schulte Roth is a former magazine editor who started in New York — *Vanity Fair, Harper's Bazaar, Details* — before moving to Atlanta to marry her southern gentleman. There she launched two luxury magazines (*Atlanta Peach, PaperCity Atlanta*) as editor-in-chief before joining the Savannah College of Art and Design (SCAD) as the Managing Director of Communications. She relocated to Asheville in 2012 where she works in the luxury travel, fashion and real estate market. She recently co-founded The Asheville Literary Society

Contributors

and Social Club in order to host local events with bestselling authors and celebrated creatives.

Kimberly Smith
Inspired by long hikes in the world's landscapes with her husband and canine best friends, Kimberly creates color-filled art that exudes nature's influence. Acrylic, watercolors, stencils, inks and chalks blend to create unique backgrounds on canvas. Her creations are then enhanced with her hand-crafted prints, fabrics, papers, recycled matter, photos and memorabilia. Kimberly's original pieces can be found in national fine art shows and galleries. Her art has been featured in over 200 collections across the nation, such as in the Hotel Allegra (Chicago), the Bali Club (Hawaii), Disney's Contemporary Hotel (Orlando) and in the Tower Hill Gallery (Michigan). Her work is found at Trackside Studios in the River Arts District in Asheville, North Carolina, and she is represented by Atomic Furnishings and Design. Instagram: @sunfinstudio

Porter Taylor
Porter Taylor is the author of three books: *Are You Persuaded? In and Out of Being a Bishop*, *To Dream as God Dreams* and *From Anger to Zion: An Alphabet of Faith.* He is the retired Episcopal Bishop of the Diocese of western North Carolina. Porter earned a BA from UNC, a Master in English from the University of South Carolina, A master's in divinity from The University of the South, and a PhD in Literature and Theology from Emory University. He and his wife, Jo, and their dog, Sadie, live in Asheville.

Raphaella Vaisseau
A self-supporting artist for over 27 years, Raphaella Vaisseau inspires with words and color, creating art she hopes will touch your heart in sweet and wonderful ways. In her work, she offers you color to heal and bless you, art as a catalyst for feeling and knowing your

extraordinary self-worth, inspiration to assist you in staying focused on your goals while uplifting you to greater heights and deeper understanding, and the words to say what's in your heart to people you love. Raphaella is committed to making a positive difference in the lives of everyone touched by her Heartful Art. heartfulart.com

Heather West
Heather West is a 5th-generation native of Madison County, North Carolina. She grew up in a family whitewater rafting business and has centered her life around the ancient waters of western North Carolina. Heather has been with Hot Springs Resort and Spa for 19 years.

Anja B. Woody
Anja B. Woody grew up in Hickory, North Carolina and has always loved the mountains. She has many happy summer memories of exploring the area near Blowing Rock, North Carolina, where her grandparents had a cabin. A Physician Assistant for 40 years, she has lived in Swannanoa, North Carolina for more than 30 years.

Endnotes

[1] "Storm Summary Message," The Weather Prediction Center, National Centers for Environmental Prediction, accessed November 2024, https://www.wpc.ncep.noaa.gov/storm_summaries/storm23/stormsum_6.html

[2] "NOWData," National Weather Service, National Oceanic and Atmospheric Administration, accessed November 2024, https://www.weather.gov/wrh/Climate?wfo=sew

[3] French Broad River at Asheville NC – 03451500 Gage Height, United States Geological Survey, accessed January 2025, https://waterdata.usgs.gov/monitoring-location/03451500/#dataTypeId=continuous-00065-0&showMedian=false&startDT=2024-09-25&endDT=2024-10-05

[4] French Broad River near Fletcher NC – 03447687 Gage Height, United States Geological Survey, accessed January 2025, https://waterdata.usgs.gov/monitoring-location/03447687/#showMedian=false&dataTypeId=continuous-00065-0&startDT=2024-09-15&endDT=2024-10-05

[5] Swannanoa River at Biltmore NC – 03451000 Gage Height, United States Geological Survey, accessed January 2024, https://waterdata.usgs.gov/monitoring-location/03451000/#dataTypeId=continuous-00065-0&showMedian=false&startDT=2024-09-26&endDT=2024-10-05

[6] Rick Jervis et al, "Heroes and Heartbreak: 36 Hours of Hell During Helene's Historic Floods," *USAToday*, October 30, 2024, https://www.usatoday.com/story/news/investigations/2024/10/30/helene/75823281007/#:~:text=As%20Helene%27s%20outer%20bands%20raked,23%2C400%20cubic%20feet%20per%20second

[7] Hurricane Helene Landslides Observation Dashboard, United States Geological Survey, accessed December 2024, https://www.arcgis.com/apps/dashboards/01b4f51fc0b64002bf7722a9acfc181d

[8] "Hurricane Helene Storm Related Fatalities," North Carolina Department of Health and Human Services, accessed January 2025, https://www.ncdhhs.gov/assistance/hurricane-helene-recovery-resources/hurricane-helene-storm-related-fatalities

[9] Josh Kelly, "Managing the Nantahala-Pisgah National Forest for Its Unique Biodiversity," accessed November 2024, https://mountaintrue.org/managing-the-nantahala-pisgah-national-forest-for-its-unique-biodiversity/

[10] "US Forest Service Releases Update on Helene's Impact to Ecosystem, Infrastructure", United States Department of Agriculture, accessed November 2024,
https://www.fs.usda.gov/detail/nfsnc/news-events/?cid=FSEPRD1213500

[11] Will Hoffman, "Clean Water Has Returned to Asheville After Helene, City Say; Boil Water Advisory Lifted," *Asheville Citizen Times*, updated November 19, 2024, https://www.citizen-times.com/story/news/local/2024/11/18/asheville-clean-water-returned-potable-city-says-lead-testing-underway/76405513007/

[12] Andrew Jones, " 'We Are Having People Go in Buckets': Mission Hospital Lacks Water, Faces Waves of Patients," *Asheville Watchdog*, October 1, 2024,
  https://avlwatchdog.org/we-are-having-people-go-in-buckets-mission-hospital-lacks-water-faces-waves-of-patients/

[13] Governor Roy Cooper, "Hurricane Helene Recovery: Revised Damage and Needs Assessment," December 13, 2024
  https://www.osbm.nc.gov/hurricane-helene-dna/open

[14] "Duke Energy Committed to Ongoing Rebuild in Western N.C., Thanks Carolina Customers for Patience and Support Following Helene", Duke Energy, October 8, 2024
  https://news.duke-energy.com/releases/duke-energy-committed-to-ongoing-rebuild-in-western-n-c-thanks-carolinas-customers-for-patience-and-support-following-helene

[15] "Communications Status Report for Areas Affected by Hurricane Helene," Federal Communications Commission, October 9, 2024,
  https://docs.fcc.gov/public/attachments/DOC-406403A1.pdf

[16] Governor Roy Cooper, "Hurricane Helene Recovery Federal Funding Request", November 13, 2024,
  https://www.osbm.nc.gov/hurricane-helene-recovery-federal-funding-needs/open

[17] "Designated Disasters: Area 4827," Federal Emergency Management Agency, North Carolina Disaster Declaration as of October 15, 2024,

https://www.fema.gov/disaster/4827/designated-areas#:~:text=PA%2DC-,Alexander%20(County),Mitchell%20(County)

[18] Cary Mock, "How Hurricane Helene Became a Deadly Disaster Across Six States," University of South Carolina, October 7, 2024, https://sc.edu/uofsc/posts/2024/10/conversation-hurricane-helene-deadly-disaster-six-states.php#:~:text=Helene's%20size%20was%20an%20important,both%20at%20about%2015%20feet

[19] "North Carolina Hurricane Helene Recovery – Debris Removal Progress," United States Army Corps of Engineers, accessed December 20, 2024, https://www.saw.usace.army.mil/Missions/HeleneResponse/

[20] "How Big Is 1,500,000 Cubic Yards?" The Measure of Things, accessed December 2024, https://www.themeasureofthings.com/results.php?comp=volume&unit=cy&amt=1500000

[21] "Billion-Dollar Weather and Climate Disasters: Time Series," National Centers for Environmental Information, accessed January 2025, https://www.ncei.noaa.gov/access/billions/time-series

www.ingramcontent.com/pod-product-compliance
Lightning Source LLC
Chambersburg PA
CBHW051631120626
46551CB00014B/2026